Always There:
The African-American Presence
in American Quilts

Always There:
The African-American Presence
in American Quilts

Cuesta Benberry

Forewords by Jonathan Holstein
and Shelly Zegart

The Kentucky Quilt Project, Inc.

ISBN # 1-880-584-02-6

This catalogue was published in conjunction with the exhibition
"Always There: The African-American Presence in American Quilts"
produced by The Kentucky Quilt Project, Inc.
as part of "Louisville Celebrates the American Quilt"
Exhibition Curator - Cuesta Benberry
Museum of History and Science, Louisville, Kentucky
February 7, 1992 - March 31, 1992

Table of Contents

Foreword

On a sticky July morning of 1989 I was sitting in a meeting room in New York with Shelly Zegart, a director of The Kentucky Quilt Project, and other equally informed quilt aficionados. There were scholars, museum professionals, quilt collectors and dealers, people interested in African-American culture. All had come in a month when basic survival instincts instruct one to be anyplace but New York to hear a series of talks on the subject of African-American quilts. The seminar had been planned to accompany the opening of the exhibition of ante-bellum, black-made quilts, *Stitched From the Soul*, but was not confined to that subject matter. An African-American quiltmaker described and interpreted her quilts, a scholar discussed the relation of some southern African-American quilts to textiles from an African tradition, others discussed other matters.

Then came Cuesta Benberry. We had first met when she and I had, some months earlier with Imelda DeGraw, juried the Arizona Quilt Project's exhibition. I had admired then Cuesta's lively intelligence and her grasp of areas of quilt information which were obscure to me. (Cuesta has done much work with primary sources as yet little used because of their relative inaccessibility and a limited understanding in the field of their importance.) I enjoyed the way she thought about quilts, fully aware of their aesthetics, seeing them also in their historical contexts. I wanted to hear more of her thoughts.

What she said on that July day in New York was the most interesting thing I had heard about quilts in a long time. It was simple, as are so many wonderful and correct notions. While, she said, investigations of the byways of African-American quiltmaking are interesting and valuable, isn't it time we looked clearly at the mainstream? What has been the overall African-American involvement with American quiltmaking?

As I thought about this over the next few months, I realized that black quilts were being categorized and described as if there were an underlying aesthetic, work method or other intrinsic qualities which should allow us to identify them through stylistic or technical means. Common sense dictates otherwise. The determination grew. If ever I had a chance to help Cuesta do an exhibition which would present her point of view, one, it seemed to me, so correct and important to quilt scholarship, I would do that.

It did not take long for the chance to arrive, unbidden. When Shelly Zegart called me to discuss remounting *Abstract Design in American Quilts* in Louisville, one of my first questions was, could we do more? Could we do Cuesta's exhibition, also?

Shelly, to her great credit, took just a few seconds to think about it and said she thought we could. So there we were. And here it is.

It pleases me enormously that I have had a small part in the enterprise. It pleases me greatly that I have had a chance to work more with Cuesta, to correspond, discuss, because of *Always There*. And it knocks me out that there happened, because of this project, one of those serendipitous things which seem often to occur around quilts. Cuesta had always said, as we discussed the exhibition, that while there were well-documented pre-Civil War African-American quilts and many from the 1920s on, there was a half-century span in which little could be found; there wasn't much known and available from that era to include in an exhibition of firmly-documented material. A chance remark at a friend's house (Why are you spending all that time in Louisville? Well, I'm working on this quilt project, blah blah) got me to George Wilbourn, the keeper with his sister Vera Holzman of the Perkins family quilts and history. These quilts, from the late nineteenth and early twentieth centuries, are an essential part of this exhibition and the developing historical picture of African-American quiltmaking. Cuesta said, "Well, Jon, the Lord caused his face to shine upon you that day." And so He did.

The exhibition is timely. It was badly needed. And while all who labor in this gentle vineyard know Cuesta by her works, it gives a long overdue, more public recognition to the scholarship, thinking and influence of one of the preeminent researchers in the field of American quilts.

Jonathan Holstein

Foreword

In 1990 Jon Holstein and I were talking about the possibility of re-creating the 1971 exhibition, *Abstract Design in American Quilts*, which originated at the Whitney Museum of American Art in New York and was then seen in other museums here and abroad for the next three years. As we discussed its continuing ramifications in the quilt world, we realized we were interested in a larger endeavor, perhaps a group of events which would highlight the things which had flowed from that exhibition.

It was obvious we would need a good organization to create and manage such an extensive project. Fortunately, one existed — The Kentucky Quilt Project, Inc. Eleanor Miller and I had, with others, organized The Kentucky Quilt Project in 1981 to survey Kentucky's quilts. Besides implementing the first state quilt survey, The Kentucky Quilt Project presented an exhibition drawn from the most interesting of the quilts found, *Kentucky Quilts: 1800-1900* which appeared first at the Louisville Museum of History and Science in 1983 and at twelve museums thereafter under the auspices of the Smithsonian Institution Traveling Exhibition Service. A catalogue of the same title accompanied the exhibition. Jon's association with the project began when he was asked to write an introduction and quilt commentaries for the catalogue. In 1984 he joined Eleanor and myself as a director of The Kentucky Quilt Project.

After determining we would do a celebration with *Abstract Design in American Quilts* as our anchoring event, our next thought was Cuesta Benberry: an exhibition illustrating her thinking about African-American quilts must be part of it. I had heard Cuesta speak several times over the years on quilt subjects as diverse as W.P.A. Quilts and "Quilts of Struggle" from Soweto, South Africa. Yet her extensive work in the area of African-American quilts was not known to me until a conference in New York in 1989 on black quiltmaking. I heard her speak there about the need to examine African-American quilts in the mainstream. What Cuesta said that day changed my perception of African-American quilts. I then began to read some articles Cuesta had written on the subject, including "The Story-Tellers: African-American Quilts Come to the Fore" in *Quilter's Newsletter Magazine*. It seemed to me that Cuesta's perspective should be known to a larger audience and that a wider view of African-American quiltmaking was long overdue.

Gaining a clear perspective of particular quilts is a familiar issue for The Kentucky Quilt Project. A main goal of the first project was to examine Kentucky's quilts in relation to the main body of American quiltmaking. Until the survey, the accepted image of the Kentucky quilt was a thick country quilt in a mountain cabin. They never appeared.

Instead, the survey showed that Kentucky quilts had both some singular characteristics peculiar to them and traits they shared with the mainstream. Some of America's most elegant quilts were of Kentucky origin.

Similarly, the African-American quilts we expected to find in a state with a significant black population and a long-standing quiltmaking tradition, did not appear. Where were they? We found several answers. First, many black families were reluctant to come forward with their quilts, feeling they weren't "good" enough. Also, when they did appear, their family histories were usually lacking. We felt the reason for this was the frequent dislocation of many African-American families and the difficulty of maintaining social continuity and history under those circumstances.

A number of recent exhibitions and seminars had focused on issues of black quiltmaking, and serious issues of scholarship had been raised. An exhibition in Kentucky illustrating Cuesta's viewpoint would, we felt, both further knowledge of African-American quilts on a national level and bring to Kentucky's citizens an extraordinary chance to see the African-American quilt heritage in better perspective. Once we had made that decision, the second one was obvious: These goals could be furthered by a public discussion among scholars of the major issues in African-American quilt history. So a conference, "The African-American and the American Quilt," was planned and became a part of the Celebration.

Cuesta and others have worked valiantly for a more balanced view of African-American quilts. This exhibition, the first overall view of the subject, is a summation of years of research. The facts are not easy to find. When early quilt histories were written, African-Americans were seldom included, as black domestic life was of little interest to scholars and writers. This clearly is no longer true, and we hope *Always There* will encourage African-American families to examine and bring forward their quilting histories. This will enable Cuesta and her colleagues to continue building a comprehensive history of the African-American contribution to American quiltmaking.

Shelly Zegart

Introduction

For over thirty years quilt research has been my absorbing interest. I studied quilts made in the United States, Canada and Europe, wrote numerous quilt history essays, and also served as the history and research editor for one of the early quilt magazines. It was not, however, until I concentrated my investigations on African-American quilt history that my interest became a passion. The motivation was my belief that, as an African-American woman, I could make a significant contribution to the larger subject of black history in America. As I researched the relatively obscure topic of African-American quiltmaking, truly virgin territory, I was challenged beyond any of my previous efforts. Those years of study have now culminated in the exhibition *Always There: The African-American Presence in American Quilts*.

African-Americans have made quilts in this land continuously from the late eighteenth century to the present. Yet their work is conspicuously absent from the many published accounts of American quilt history. One purpose of our exhibition is to remedy this omission. The organization is chronological and historical, in time, place and circumstance, a look at the entire range of African-American quiltmaking experiences. Quilts were made in the ante-bellum period by both slave and free blacks; later, by middle class blacks and impoverished blacks; by educated blacks and those without educational advantages; by women, men, and children; by folk artists and trained artists; and by persons who lived in the North, the South, the Midwest and the West. Examples of quilts from most of these socio-economic groups, and from most geographic regions and times, have been located for the exhibition. Apparent in the works of some African-American artists, poets, novelists and painters who pursued other avenues of expression, were manifestations of exposure to family quilting traditions. A narration of these related expressions is included in the exhibition catalogue. Not only did countless African-Americans participate in American quiltmaking, but blacks also had an early role in spreading the American style of quiltmaking beyond the borders of the United States. Artifacts related to this foreign dissemination of the quiltmaking craft are included in the exhibition.

During a broadcast of the series "Quilting II by Penny McMorris," I predicted, ". . . Afro-American quilts will be to the 1980s what Amish quilts were to the 1970s — objects of intense interest and scholarly investigations." Why, after many years of near invisibility, have African-American quilts now become so engrossing to art historians, folklorists, ethnologists and quilt historians? Several factors, products of the times, are the basis of the current explorations of African-American quilts. A result of the 1960s-1970s civil rights movement and attendant upheaval was the phenomenal growth of black studies programs in various American schools, from elementary to university levels. Black history received the seal of approval from much, but not all, of the academic community. Attempts to implement black studies programs were often met with hostility, sometimes subtle, more often blatant. The guaranteed result of these heated controversies was enormous publicity. Black history attained the status of a legitimate discipline and would not disappear.

Concomitant with the blacks' civil rights actions was the women's or feminist movement. Feminist concerns were the catalyst for a number of women's history studies, including the history of African-American women. In their consciousness-raising essays, feminist authors such as Patricia Mainardi, Rachel Maines, Sally Garoutte and Elaine Hedges emphasized the historical and artistic significance of the patch-work quilt. In her essay "Piecing and Writing," Elaine Showalter wrote, "The patchwork quilt has become one of the most central images in the feminist lexicon." Feminist involvement with patchwork quilt history represented only one segment of the massive participation of Americans in the late twentieth century quilt revival that was occurring. Never before in America had a quilt revival reached this magnitude, not even in the 1930s. The new quilt movement of the last quarter of the twentieth century was stimulated by events such as the 1971 Whitney Museum of American Art quilt exhibition, the subsequent quilt exhibitions at other notable museums, the publication and national distribution of periodicals solely devoted to the subject of quilts, the establishment of a multitude of local quilt guilds, the convening of national quilt conferences and seminars, and the participation of antique dealers, who responded to a growing market for old quilts. Further impetus came from ecologists, who espoused the need to return to plain, self-reliant and healthy living. A new cadre of quilt historians, fostered by the resurgence of interest, treated the study of patchwork quilts as a scholarly discipline and not as a minor adjunct to the studies of art history, folklore or women's studies. These quilt historians were determined to produce an accurate history of quilts, to document fully quilts and quiltmakers past and present, and to explore topics never before researched in the context of quilt history.

A fourth factor, and one that had perhaps the most direct impact on the scholars' desire to investigate African-American quilts, was the advent of the 1976 bicentennial commemoration, an event accompanied by a celebration of ethnic diversity in our multicultural society. Certain quilt historians had as a priority the investigation of the ways the quilts of various ethnic groups connected to the social, political and economic conditions of their lives in America. Extensive examinations were conducted on the quilts and quilt-related works of the Amish, the Mennonites, Seminole Indians, Hawaiians, Southwestern Hispanic-Americans, the newly settled Hmong, and African-Americans.

High drama was associated with the early research of African-American quilts. Scholars located a small group of quilts profoundly different visually from the accepted aesthetic of traditional American patchwork quilts. These idiosyncratic quilts from black women of rural southern and similar backgrounds were examined closely for stylistic variances, construction techniques, fabric color choices and symbolic design references. Most exciting of all was a linkage between the black American quilts and African design traditions, believed to indicate an unconscious cultural memory in the quiltmakers of their far-away mother-land. African-American quilts became one of America's newest forms of exotica. Continued scrutinization of the quilts resulted in the promulgation of a number of theories which were immediately accepted as fact. Visual criteria for recognizing African-American quilts (stitch length, asymmetrical organization of quilt patches, size of the patches, frequent use of bright colors) were devised. Long established canons of quilt history research, such as determining the quiltmaker's identity, the quilt's provenance, date of making and fabric content, were no longer deemed essential. One needed only apply the recently-created visual criteria to identify with certainty quilts of African-American origin.

Such an extremely myopic view of African-American quilts made many scholars of black history and quilt history researchers uneasy. How could this small sample of late twentieth century African-American quilts represent in its entirety the contribution of thousands of black quiltmakers working at the craft over two centuries? Would the history of blacks in America affirm that they had been a monolithic group without different experiences, environments, customs, and beliefs which would affect their creative efforts? What should one think of African-American quilts, made over such a long period of time, that did *not* conform to the aesthetics-based identification? The casual answer that African-American quilts not in compliance with the criteria were simply copies of white-made, traditional Euro-American quilts was unacceptable. That reply was of dubious historical validity, a facile assessment derived from the popular culture, of American quilt history. What were we seeing here? How could the quiltworks of hundreds of thousands of African-Americans of many regions, times and circumstances be correctly assessed in a conjectural, non-statistically based one sentence answer? Where was the evidence to sustain that broad conclusion? More and more questions about African-American quilts emerged as quilt historians realized findings gathered in these early studies of black-made quilts had been extrapolated far beyond what the evidence would legitimately support.

Further research began to place African-American quilts in the larger context of black history. There was a need to dispel certain myths that had developed about African-American quilts, to examine some of the influences on these creations, to portray the enormous diversity that characterized black-made quilts and, when possible, give voice to the quiltmakers themselves. It is important to listen to what African-American quiltmakers say about their work and to give them credence, whether or not their comments coincide with researchers' theories and interpretations. It is certainly not useful to view African-American quilts merely as isolated folk art objects, divorced from the lives of blacks and the social, political and economic conditions under which they have lived. A small percentage of African-American quilts are visually exotic; the majority are not. More important than aesthetic considerations, or a discerned decorative imagery, the quilts represent a diverse body of work by an ethnic group distinguished for its lengthy participation in American quiltmaking. The record should so state, and then African-American quilts and quiltmakers will begin to attain their rightful place in American quilt history. The exhibition *Always There: The African-American Presence in American Quilts* explores the historical chronology, the characteristic diversity of African-American quilts and the roles played by black quiltmakers in America.

Cuesta Benberry

Always There: The African-American Presence in American Quilts

Although quilting has been practiced for centuries on the continents of Asia, Africa, Europe, and North America, quilt history has not until very recently been considered a legitimate area of study. There were a number of reasons for quilt history's lack of scholarly status among which were gender bias (quilting was perceived in America as solely a woman's concern and occupation) and class bias (in some foreign lands, it was seen as exclusively an upper class pursuit; in others, a lower). Quilts were also regarded as a minor folk art not worthy of serious or lengthy investigation.

This biased perception has changed as scholars have understood and accepted the centuries old, worldwide participation of millions of people in making quilts. The study of quilt history has assumed a more creditable position as a valid branch of knowledge and an aggregate record of specific human endeavors. Quilt history is not simply an adjunct to art history, folk life studies, ethnology or anthropology although the methodologies of those disciplines can greatly enhance the study of quilt history. The recognition of folk art as a subject worthy of study began in America only in the early part of the twentieth century. So it is not surprising that quilt history, considered a female-dominated narrative, would not receive sustained, scholarly examination until the latter part of the century. Traditionally, historians have first sought factual information and would subsequently devise historical theories and interpretations based on those facts. Quilt historians are following the path of tradition.

The exhibition *Always There: The African-American Presence in American Quilts* is primarily concerned with the presentation of factual information. I believe it is essential to convey initially a sense of the lengthy and continuous participation of black people in quiltmaking in America, supported with accurate data. Adhering to this method of historical investigation prevents a too-hasty, anachronistic interpretation of the historical record. A procedure, in which the quilts of a small group of black quiltmakers from a limited time frame are selected, examined for common characteristics, conclusions reached, interpretations of the works devised, and extrapolations from these made to all African-American quilts of all times, is at odds with the accepted method of historical inquiry. Unfortunately, such premature assumptions have been made and have gained wide credence. Scholars familiar with the utilization of small scientific samplings that can, at times, predict with a fair degree of accuracy certain human behaviors appear to be comfortable when similar shortcut methods of investigation are applied to complicated historical data. I believe those procedures are meaningless when applied to determining creative characteristics of large groups, such as the millions of black people who have lived in this land for nearly four hundred years. Human creativity has so many variables, it is beyond the purview of small scientific samplings. Yet many persons have accepted the erroneous assumptions of these skewed studies and are certain they can identify African-American quilts on sight. They are often wrong but are never in doubt.

Chapter 1:
Slave-Made Quilts in Ante-Bellum America

As with all African-American quilts, a compelling reason to research slave-made quilts was to ascertain the role of black quiltmaking in American quilt history. To paraphrase Dr. W. E. B. DuBois, these long-ignored quilts represented the works of "a wholly submerged group, the world has saved all too little of [their] authentic record and tried to forget or ignore even the little saved." [1] Quiltmaking by enslaved blacks was widespread as examples of slave-made quilts have been found in every former slave-holding state in the Union. A sizeable percentage of extant slave quilts are in the possession of white slave-owners' descendants; so much of the information associated with the quilts would come necessarily from the oral histories provided by the quilts' present owners. To balance these sources, primary historical documents (first-hand slave narratives recorded in the ante-bellum period and later interviews with former slaves in the post-bellum era and the 1930s Works Progress Administration [W. P. A.] Federal Writers' Projects) were consulted. The dichotomy of views regarding slaves' lives between black Americans (as recorded in the slaves' narratives) and white Americans (as told in the oral histories supplied by descendants of the slave owners) was apparent. Frequently the opinions are widely divergent. The necessity of recording the viewpoints of slaves in their own words was expressed in the introduction to a compilation of slave narratives:

> Although the slave system in the United States has been studied as thoroughly as any institution of modern times, until recently few scholars have examined the testimony of its black victims. Presumably they were considered too unobservant, too subjective, and their views too poorly expressed to be of much value to the historian or sociologist. For the longest time the intellectual arbiters of the slave system were those who profited from it, their friends and their relatives. [2]

The voluminous entries of slave life histories in the W. P. A. Federal Writers' Project's collections contained numerous citations of quiltmaking by enslaved blacks. Regardless of how rich a vein of information the W. P. A. Federal Writers' Project proved to be, it was not an infallible reference source, as the W. P. A. slave narratives were tainted both in methodologies and substance. John Blassingame's brilliant critique of the W. P. A. slave narratives, noting their deficiencies, is a warning to be wary when utilizing these testimonies. [3] Other sources, such as the ante-bellum slave and early post-bellum former slaves' autobiographies, the first-person slave accounts in abolitionist journals and later newspapers, need also be used with caution. The wisest policy would be to consult all types of slave life histories without complete reliance on one kind because, as Eugene Genovese wrote, ". . . all the sources are treacherous and . . . no 'definitive' study has been written or ever will be written." [4]

The Emancipation Proclamation of 1863 freed only the slaves who lived in areas in rebellion against the Union. Emancipation brought overwhelming joy to many slaves and bewilderment to others. Countless slaves' lives were unchanged as they were not told of their new freedom by their slave masters and remained in virtual peonage. Union soldiers, in certain areas, went from farm to farm, household to household, advising the slaves they were no longer to be held in bondage. There are accounts of slaves being victimized by invading Yankee soldiers as well as by their former masters, as Sam York, Arkansas, related in the following W. P. A. narrative:

> Mother had lots of nice things, quilts and things, and kept 'em in a chest in her little old shack. One day a Yankee soldier climbed in the back window and took some of the quilts. He rolled 'em up and was walking out of the yard when Mother saw him and said, "Why, you nasty stinking rascal! You say you come down here to fight for the niggers, and now you're stealing from 'em." He said, "You're a godamn liar. I'm fighting for $14 a month and the Union." [5]

During the compilation of the W. P. A. narratives, numerous aged black former slaves, who were interviewed, exhibited docility and great deference toward their white interviewers, who frequently lived in the same areas. Blacks were intimidated by the segregated southern caste system, firmly in place in the 1930s. Not so, Thomas Hall, an unintimidated black respondent quoted in the excerpt from his W. P. A. narrative:

> Lincoln got the praise for freeing us, but did he do it? . . .
> Lincoln done but little for the Negro race and from a living stand-point, nothing . . . When I think of slavery, it makes me mad. I do not believe in giving you my story, 'cause with all the promises that have been made, the Negro is still in a bad way in the United States, no matter in what part he lives. It's all the same . . . You are going around to get a story of slave conditions and the persecutions of

*Negroes before the Civil War and the economic conditions concern-
ing them since that war. You should have known before this late day
all about that. Are you going to help us? No! You are only helping
yourself. You say that my story may be put into a book, that you
are from the Federal Writers' Project. Well, the Negro will not get
anything out of it, no matter where you are from. Harriet Beecher
Stowe wrote* Uncle Tom's Cabin. *I didn't like her book and I hate
her. No matter where you are from I don't want you to write my
story 'cause the white folks have been and are now and always will
be against the Negro.* [6]

Years prior to the installation of the W. P. A. Federal Writers'
Project, in the late nineteenth and early twentieth centuries, African-
American journalists wrote firsthand accounts of slaves' lives under
bondage. An 1893 graduate of Radcliffe College, African-American
Mary White Ovington, became an outstanding journalist. She interviewed former slaves, including "Uncle Ben" in Alabama who told what
happened at the time of Emancipation:

*When the gran' ole freedom bell rung I see the niggers goin' to the
city; yes, and I see the white folks cut off women's breasts. They
was mad, jes' mad, an' they wouldn't let the niggers back on the
plantations not then. The women 'ud have to sleep in their quilts by
the road. Um, Um, it was terrible. I hasn't half told you how
terrible it was.* [7]

Africans brought to America were unfamiliar with the bed
quilt but had knowledge both of the techniques used in making a quilt
(piecing, applique, embroidery) and in weaving cloth. For many of the
enslaved, the transition to quiltmaking was accomplished with relative
ease. Extant slave-made pieced, appliqued, embroidered, whole-cloth,
broderie perse, and reverse appliqued quilts are visible evidence of the
extraordinary proficiency of the makers. When slave-made quilts displaying a high degree of technical skill are located, apocryphal statements are
frequently made that such quilts are not true African-American quilts;
that the quilts are reflections of the white slave mistresses' ideas and
instructions, and black slaves were merely the mechanical means of
completing her projects. Assertions such as these tend to trivialize the
quiltworks of self-taught slave seamstresses, or those who were taught to
sew by other female slaves, the mothers, grandmothers, friends, or slave

seamstresses specifically bought and brought into a household because of their sewing skills. Often, such sewing abilities were prominently advertised on slave sale handbills. Certain slave mistresses did teach their slaves to sew while other mistresses had neither the inclination nor the ability to teach their slaves to sew.

Historians tend to make assumptions about slave sewing that do not take into account the complexities of the slave mistress-slave seamstress relationships and variations on the divisions of labor from household to household. Labor configurations included the slave seamstress, who performed a sewing task alone or in concert with other slaves; the slave mistress, who reserved for herself specific sewing tasks; and the joint sewing projects of mistress and slaves. A rare, documented study of black and white women working together on textile production is contained in the exhaustive investigations of Mary Lohrenz pertaining to the white woman, L. E. Black, and the slave woman, Chany, on a Tennessee plantation in the ante-bellum South.[8] A glimpse into the intimate household production of the legendary Mount Vernon plantation, home of George Washington, is revealed in a 1799 letter written by Mrs. Edward Carrington, describing the sewing room of Martha Washington:

> *My mornings are spent charmingly . . . then we repair to the old*
> *lady's [Martha Washington] room, which is precisely on the style of*
> *our good old Aunt's — that is to say nicely fixed up for all sorts of*
> *work . . . on one side sits the chambermaid with her knitting, on the*
> *other a little colored pet learning to sew, an old decent woman with*
> *her table and shears cutting out the negroes winter clothes, while the*
> *good old lady directs them all, incessantly knitting herself, and*
> *pointing out to me several pairs of nice colored stockings and gloves*
> *she had just finished, and presenting me with a pair half done, she*
> *begs me to finish and wear for her sake.* [9]

Another letter from Mrs. Martha Stewart Wilson relates the magnitude of the Mount Vernon home production when the writer quotes, "Mrs. Washington told how it became necessary to make their own domestic cloth, a task at which sixteen spinning wheels were kept constantly busy."[10] To assess, even partially, the works of the slave seamstress, there must also be taken into account such factors as the nature of the sewing task when it involved the home production of cloth, the sewing of slaves' clothing from purchased "Negro cloth" from northern mills,[11] the making of quilts for bedding, and the size of the slave owner's household, including the resident slaves.

Harriet Tubman, an escaped slave from Maryland and one of the most courageous and daring conductors on the Underground Railroad, led over 300 enslaved men, women and children to freedom in the North, "without," she said, "ever losing a passenger." Tubman, who could not read or write, dictated her life story to her white friend, Sarah Bradford. Tubman's memoirs were published in the 1869 book *Scenes in the Life of Harriet Tubman* and in the 1886 book *Harriet, the Moses of her People*. The narratives disclosed that Harriet Tubman was a self-taught slave quiltmaker who made a patchwork quilt in 1843 prior to her marriage to John Tubman, a free black, in 1844. Harriet Tubman cherished her quilt and called it the most beautiful thing she ever owned. When she was aided by a white woman in her initial 1849 escape from Maryland and had no money to pay the woman, Harriet Tubman gave her the beloved quilt. Later Tubman biographers award-winning Ann Petry (1956) and Kate McMullan (1991), by consulting primary sources, were able to record Harriet Tubman's fond and recurring memories of that quilt during her harrowing Underground Railroad adventures, her hazardous spy escapades in the Civil War, and on to the end of her life.[12]

Stories, whether mythical or factual, constitute a colorful part of quilt lore. A story, as yet undocumented, tells of quilts in the "Jacob's Ladder" pattern (renamed "Underground Railroad") hung outside houses as a signal to passengers on the Underground Railroad that the homes were safe havens for the fearful travelers. The origin of the renamed "Underground Railroad" quilt pattern was attributed to the Western Reserve (Ohio) by Ruth Finley, and to western Kentucky by Carrie Hall.[13] Both areas were well-traveled routes on the Underground Railroad. In another story from quilt lore, a sign of secure shelter on the Underground Railroad was a "Phrygian Cap" or "Liberty Cap" hanging outside a home. Whether the stories are true or simply romantic myths I am unable to say at this time. Experience has taught that some quilt stories prove upon investigations to be true while others prove untrue, the products of over-active imaginations.

It has also been said the "North Star" quilt pattern was inspired by the escaped slaves' travels via the Underground Railroad. Harriet Tubman did use the North Star as a nighttime guide on her forays into the South to bring slaves to freedom. Frederick Douglass, the most prominent African-American abolitionist in the anti-slavery movement, published a newspaper entitled *The North Star*. I do not know, however, the origin of the "North Star" quilt pattern or whether it was connected to the slaves' quest for freedom.

One year after Harriet Tubman made her treasured quilt, an anonymous slave stitched a pieced quilt in "The Reel" pattern (Figure #1) on a plantation near Sedalia, Missouri. Pieced in an assortment of brown calicoes with a single red center block, the quilt has the date "1844" stitched in red tiny cross-stitch on the reverse lining. Originally, "The Reel" was one of a pair of identical quilts made by the same slave. Both quilts were offered for sale in the 1930s and at that time the present owner, Mrs. William Miller, purchased the one in the exhibition. "The Reel" quilt gained a measure of fame when it was in the 1969 traveling needlework exhibition, *Stitched in Time*, sponsored by the Hallmark Gallery, New York, and *Woman's Day Magazine*. One of the finest, most comprehensive needlework exhibitions ever mounted, it contained a celebrity section with pieces by Pearl Bailey, Andy Warhol, Queen Mary of England, Mary Martin, Sylvia Sidney, Joanne Woodward, Edye Gormé, "Rosie" Grier, Joan Fontaine, Julie Nixon Eisenhower and other celebrities. Early United States history was represented by embroidery from Martha Washington and her daughter, Nelly Custis, and by a nineteenth century beaded cradle from the Kiowa tribe of Oklahoma. "The Reel" quilt was in rare company with a nineteenth century Baltimore album quilt, Gypsy Rose Lee's crazy quilt, a red and yellow Hawaiian quilt, a Freedom Quilting Bee Quilt from Gees Bend, Alabama, and sixty-one blocks from the Carrie Hall collection, plus other notable quilts. I saw the exhibition and noted that "The Reel" quilt visually held its own amidst an astounding array of needlework items.[14]

Anonymous also was the slave quiltmaker who constructed the "Original Whig Rose" quilt, circa 1860 (Figure #2). It is known that the slave quiltmaker lived on a plantation belonging to the White family and lived near Richmond, Kentucky. When the White's daughter married and moved west to Missouri in a covered wagon, the "Original Whig Rose" quilt accompanied the newlyweds. Whether the quilt's name, "Original Whig Rose," indicated the political sentiments of the White family is not known. However, the title of the Kentucky slave-made quilt, "Original Whig Rose," seemed appropriate as the famous Kentucky statesman, Henry Clay, leader of the Whig party, was the organization's candidate for President in 1844. The Whigs' strength was diminished through infighting when the northern anti-slavery faction, called the "Conscience Whigs," opposed the southern pro-slavery faction, called the "Cotton Whigs." The dissolution of the Whig Party resulted from the passage in 1854 of the Kansas-Nebraska Bill. Northern Whigs joined the newly formed Republican Party; the southern Whigs joined first the Know-Nothing Party and eventually were absorbed by the Southern Democratic Party.

Despite being one hundred fifty years old, the slave-made appliqued "Tulip" quilt (Figure #3) from a plantation in Virginia has retained its bright, fresh look. A light, airy feeling of movement on the thirty-block quilt was achieved by placing each slender tulip design diagonally on a straight sashed set. Placed on a light background, the graceful red tulip design, with slightly different centers on alternate squares, was repeated throughout the quilt. Ann, a sixteen-year-old slave who belonged to Captain and Mrs. William Womack, Pittsylvania County, Virginia, produced this exceptional quilt. It is now in the collection of the National Museum of American History, Smithsonian Institution, Washington, D. C.

As the majority of extant slave quilts are in the possession of the slave owners' descendants, various scholars have assumed that all of those quilts were originally made for the owners' households by slave seamstresses. Searches have been ongoing for quilts created by slaves for their own use, but few have been located. Although few quilts constructed by slaves for personal use are known, attempts have been made to assign design characteristics to this body of largely invisible work. Assertions are made that quilts slaves produced for themselves differed greatly from quilts sewn for their masters' homes.

> *They [the enslaved] make quilts for themselves and for each other . . . Since this quiltmaking occurs outside of the routine of work done for the master, and consequently emerges and matures somewhat independently of European-American interferences, it holds the potential to become a vehicle for the expression of African values. Thus an African-American quilt tradition, rich in African lore, is born.*[15]

Or even the less tentative, more firmly stated opinion:

> *Quilts were produced by Black women for utilitarian and decorative purposes in both White and Black households. Quilts made for Whites are hardly distinguishable from traditional Anglo-American ones. However, those quilts made for personal use of Blacks (very few examples survive) were designed and stitched in the African tradition.*[16]

I would concur with the statement that surviving examples of known quilts slaves made for themselves are few. I have seen a limited number of such quilts, but the specimens I examined were in traditional American patchwork quilt designs such as variations of "Nine-Patch," "Log Cabin," and "Rob Peter to Pay Paul." On the basis of this scant evidence, should I state that quilts constructed by slaves for personal use did not differ substantially from the quilts fashioned for their white owners? Given the breadth and complexity of the entire subject of quilts made by slaves for themselves, a more responsible policy for all scholars would be to forego sweeping generalizations and premature, perhaps even historically inaccurate, judgments derived from an insufficient information base.

With the advent of recent African-American quilt research, the traditional American patchwork quilt (the geometric patchwork quilt in a block configuration) began to be termed "European," "Euro-American" and "Anglo-American." Apparently, this was done to more vividly contrast American black-made quilts and white-made quilts. The terminology quickly gained widespread acceptance and usage. (I briefly participated in the fad.) On the surface, the terminology appeared to be logical and valid because more of the traditional patchwork quilts had been made by the white majority population; the quilts are familiar to most people, and quiltmaking had been introduced into America by Europeans.

Serious reflection, however, raised many questions. What was the history of European quilting prior to and at the time of the early colonists' immigration into America? How were the separate modalities of quilting and patchwork perceived in Europe? Was the patchwork quilt in a geometric block configuration the type of quilt brought to early America by the Europeans, or did the form develop in America later in the eighteenth and early nineteenth century by an evolutionary process? If the latter were true, did African-Americans participate in the development of that evolutionary process that produced what is now known as the traditional American patchwork quilt? By accepting without question the designation of the traditional American patchwork quilt as European, we effectively eliminated any role of African-Americans in the evolutionary process that marked the development of the distinctively American patchwork quilt. By denying African-Americans their part in that evolutionary process, it became easier to promulgate a spurious history of African-American quiltmaking in America. Characterizing African-Americans as mere observors of the process or copyists of the traditional

American patchwork quilt and deeming them a monolithic group whose creativity had been channeled into a single quiltmaking aesthetic resulted in an African-American quilt history filled with historical inaccuracies, opinions paraded as facts, half-truths and stereotypes. The theory that African-Americans had no participatory role in the evolution of the traditional American patchwork quilt is akin to the long-held, but now discredited, belief that the first American quilt was the unadorned crazy quilt.

1. Herbert Aptheker, ed., *A Documentary History of the Negro People in America*, (New York: The Citadel Press, 1951), Preface by W.E.B. DuBois.
2. William Lorenz Katz, ed., *Five Slave Narratives*, (New York: Arno Press and The New York Times, 1969), p. IV.
3. John W. Blassingame, ed., *Slave Testimony: Two Centuries of Letters, Speeches, Interviews and Autobiographies*, (Baton Rouge: Louisiana State University Press, 1977), pp. xlii-lx.
4. Eugene Genovese, *Roll, Jordan, Roll: The World The Slaves Made*, (New York: Vintage Books, 1974), p. 676.
5. B. A. Botkin, ed., *Lay My Burden Down: A Folk History Survey*, (Chicago: University of Chicago, 1945), p. 206.
6. Julius Lester, *To Be A Slave*, (New York: Scholastic Books, 1968), p. 156.
7. Blassingame, p. 535.
8. Mary Lohrenz, "Two Lives Intertwined on a Tennessee Plantation," *The Southern Quarterly*, (Fall 1988), pp. 72-92.
9. *Ibid.*
10. Dolores Hinson, *Quilting Manual*, (New York: Hearthside Press, 1966), p. 178.
11. Myron O. Stachiw, *Northern Industry and Southern Slavery*, (Boston: Merrimack Valley Textile Museum, 1981), exhibition guide; Vaughn L. Glasgow, "Textiles of the Louisiana Acadians," *The Magazine Antiques*, (August 1981).
12. Ann Petry, *Harriet Tubman: Conductor on the Underground Railroad*, (New York: Thomas Y. Crowell, 1955), pages 73-81; Kate McMullan, *The Story of Harriet Tubman; Conductor of the Underground Railroad*, (New York: Dell, 1991), *passim*.
13. Ruth Finley, *Old Patchwork Quilts and the Women Who Made Them*, (Philadelphia: J. B. Lippincott, 1929), p. 71; Carrie Hall and Rose Kretsinger, *The Romance of the Patchwork Quilt in America*, (Caldwell, Idaho: Caxton Printers, 1935), pp. 64-66.
14. "Major Exhibition of American Needlecraft Opens At New York Gallery — Stitched in Time: American Needlework Past and Present." (New York: Hallmark Gallery, 1969), exhibition catalogue; Jean Todd Freeman, "Stitched in Time," *Woman's Day Magazine*, (June 1969), p. 25.
15. Eli Leon, "Wrapping Home Around Me," *Rambling On My Mind: Black Folk Art of the Southwest*, (Dallas: Museum of African-American Life and Culture, 1987), p. 23.
16. Gladys-Marie Fry, *Stitched from the Soul: Slave Quilts from the Ante-Bellum South*, (New York: E. P. Dutton, 1990), p. 15.

Chapter 2:
Free Blacks in Ante-Bellum America

Information about free black quiltmakers in ante bellum America is even less accessible than data on the work of enslaved blacks. Regardless of whether free blacks were affluent, or marginally subsistent artisans and craftsmen, or recently escaped slaves living homeless and in poverty, life in ante-bellum America was fraught with peril for free persons of color. Southern black freedmen lived in constant jeopardy, subjected to Draconian invigilation and codes that compelled them to leave a slave state within one year of acquiring their freedom. Nor could they enter a slave state as free persons.

> . . . in both the South and the North there were numerous Negroes who acquired their freedom in other ways [than by being runaways]. Some were born free, some purchased their freedom, others were granted manumission by their masters.[1]

Manumissions could be set aside, and blacks, if unable to produce their manumission papers, could be re-enslaved.

> Under the terms of George Washington's will, all the slaves were to be freed after the death of his wife, Martha. However, his nephew, Supreme Court Justice Bushrod Washington, sold twenty-five of them, he claimed, to pay taxes on the estate.[2]

A "Sugar Loaf" pieced cotton quilt was made by Diana de Gadis Washington Hine, a former slave, born in 1793 at Mount Vernon, the plantation of George Washington. The Hine quilt is in the collection of the National Museum of American History, Smithsonian Institution, Washington, D. C.[3]

Notwithstanding their own precarious situations, many free blacks in the North and in the South relentlessly pursued freedom for their brothers and sisters in bondage. American history celebrates the heroic exploits of Harriet Tubman, who led over three hundred slaves to freedom.[4] Revisionist historians have attempted to discount the importance and scope of Underground Railroad operations. Nevertheless, there were numerous Underground Railroad routes. One passage went from the eastern seaboard of Maryland through Pennsylvania and on to Canada; others, from the border states across the Ohio River into Ohio and Indiana and from Missouri across the Mississippi River to Illinois or farther west to the Kansas and Nebraska territories. Funding for the Underground Railroad was provided by individual philanthropists and organizations such as the racially mixed American Anti-Slavery Society or the state Vigilance Committees. As an adjunct to the all-male American Anti-Slavery Society, free black women and white women organized the Female Anti-Slavery Society and assumed the tasks of circulating petitions, publishing tracts, providing schools for black children, and raising monies for the Underground Railroad.

The first Female Anti-Slavery Society was formed in 1834 by free black women in Salem, Massachusetts.[5] The largest and most prominent chapters of the Female Anti-Slavery Society were located in Boston and Philadelphia, while other chapters were established throughout the North. One method used by the Societies to raise monies for their endeavors was to hold Ladies' Fairs and Ladies' Bazaars. The Female Anti-Slavery Societies, given cooperation from other chapters and sometime later, generous donations from women's abolitionist groups overseas, became a powerful force in the freedom movement. Black women in the Salem Female Anti-Slavery Society assiduously supported the Ladies' Fairs held in Boston and elsewhere in New England. A report in the 20 December 1834 issue of *The Liberator*, the leading abolitionist journal, edited by William Lloyd Garrison, reviewed the Fair and made special mention of the black women of Salem.

Anti-Slavery Fair

The sale of articles for the benefit of the New England Anti-Slavery Society on Tuesday last, was more successful than any of the ladies anticipated . . . The proceeds of the sales amounted to more than three hundred dollars.

We are told the colored ladies of Salem particularly deserve thanks for the interest they took in the Fair, and the articles they sent.

We are sure that we shall not, in this instance, be charged with invidiousness when we allude to the modest and polite manners of Miss SUSAN PAUL, who sat at one of the tables, and with which the purchasers were much pleased. Although she has a colored complexion, yet, in all that constitutes female excellence, she has not her superior in the republic.[6]

Free-born Charlotte Forten (Grimke), the daughter of James Forten, wealthy Philadelphia African-American sailmaker and fervent abolitionist, enrolled in Salem Normal School to become a teacher. True to family tradition, she joined the Salem Female Anti-Slavery Society, participated in all of its activities, and met many famous persons in the abolitionist movement. She wrote in her journal:

> *Dec. 1856 — Spent the day delightfully at the Fair — Saw many beautiful things and interesting people. Had the good fortune to be made known to three of the noblest and best of women — Mesdames Chapman [Maria Weston], Follen [Elizabeth C.], and Child [Lydia Maria]. I attended to our Salem table part of the time, and then assisted Mrs. Follen.*[7]

Another entry in the Forten journal read:

> *Then went to the Fair, and saw many beautiful things . . . On Mrs. Stowe's [Harriet Beecher] table was a statuette of Uncle Tiff executed by a colored French artist.* [8]

The Ladies' Fairs and Ladies' Bazaars sold many different items, usually with abolitionist slogans and captions attached. When large contributions of articles to sell, including quilts and patchwork, came from the women's anti-slavery groups of England, Scotland, Ireland, France and Haiti, the scope of these annual events widened, so much so that their profits escalated to thousands of dollars.[9] Various writers today dismiss the abolitionists as wild-eyed zealots. Zealotry, like beauty, is in the eyes of the beholder. Female abolitionists were strong-minded, dedicated and hard-working free black women and white women organized together for the first time in American history. The occasional personality flaws of individual members do not discredit the organizations formed to pursue freedom for black people in bondage.

In an article I originally wrote for *Quilter's Newsletter Magazine*, I detailed the research involved in discovering and documenting a cradle quilt sold at a Boston Female Anti-Slavery Society Fair in 1836.[10] An article in *The Liberator* in 1837 described the quilt:

> *A cradle-quilt was made of patchwork in small stars* [on which] *was written in indelible ink:*

> *"Mother! When around your child*
> *You clasp your arms in love,*
> *And when with grateful joy you raise*
> *Your eyes to God above,*

Think of the negro mother
When her child is torn away
Sold for a little slave — oh then
For that poor mother pray!" [11]

This important 1836 quilt is presently housed in the collection of the Harrison-Grey Otis House, Society for the Preservation of New England Antiquities, Boston.

Acquiring documented records of free blacks living in the antebellum South can be daunting. Two quilt tops tentatively ascribed to free African-Americans are a case in point. The persons who made the quilts, their birthdates and where they lived are known; and one of the quilts is even date-inscribed. Yet all of this information is insufficient to determine their status, slave or free, because of the paucity of written records about southern blacks under the "peculiar institution" of slavery.

One quilt (Figure #4), donated to the Avery Institute, Charleston, South Carolina, by Mrs. Nell Houston Chisolm, wife of the grandson of the maker, was constructed by a Johanna Davis. Research conducted by the staff of Avery Institute indicated that Johanna Davis, a black woman, was born in 1832, lived in Charleston, became a skilled mantua and dressmaker, and made the broderie perse quilt between 1845 and 1853.[12] The quilt is typical of a kind of quilt popular in the greater Charleston area in mid-nineteenth century. Antique broderie perse quilts have become almost synonymous with Charleston, as have elaborate appliqued album quilts with Baltimore.[13] Johanna Davis' quilt top has a large central medallion all overlaid with cut-out chintz floral motifs. While the comment that it was most unusual then for a black quiltmaker to make a broderie perse quilt may prove to be true, we believe such assessments are premature. The study of early to mid-nineteenth century African-American quilts is in its infancy, and it is not yet possible to make definitive statements about the extent and kinds of quilts made then by blacks in a specific region such as South Carolina.

The second quilt (Figure #5), also a quilt top, is in the collection of the National Museum of American History; it, too, is tentatively attributed to a free black maker. Made by Frances M. Jolly, the quilt is signed and dated 1839; and its provenance is listed as Massachusetts or North Carolina. The quilt, a framed medallion in dark colors, is decorated with floral designs in wool, silk embroidery and wool and silk braids.[14]

1. Langston Hughes and Milton Meltzer, eds., *A Pictorial History of the Negro in America*, (New York: Crown Pub., 1963), p. 52.
2. Middleton Harris et al., eds., *The Black Book*, (New York: Random House, 1974), p. 421.
3. Smithsonian Institution, National Museum of American History, *Division of Textiles Photograph List*, (Washington, D. C., n. d.), catalogue number T. 14114.
4. Ann Petry, *Harriet Tubman: Conductor on the Underground Railroad*, (New York: Thomas Y. Crowell, 1955), p. 182.
5. Ray Allen Billington, *The Journal of Charlotte L. Forten: A Free Negro in the Slave Era*, (New York: W. W. Norton, 1953), p. 230.
6. *The Liberator*, William Lloyd Garrison, ed., "Anti-Slavery Fair," 20 December 1834. Garrison's *The Liberator* was the leading abolitionist journal of the nineteenth century. Additionally, less celebrated journals, such as Frederick Douglass' *The North Star*, *The African Repository*, and others were influential components of the proselytizing abolitionist press in ante-bellum America.
7. Billington, p. 87.
8. *Ibid.*, p. 113.
9. Cuesta Benberry, "Afro-American Slave Quilts and the British Connection," Parts 1 and 2, *America in Britain* (Bath, England: The American Museum in Britain), Fall 1987; Winter 1987.
10. *Idem*, "A Quilt Research Surprise," *Quilter's Newsletter Magazine*, (July/August 1981), pp. 34-35.
11. *The Liberator*, 2 January 1837.
12. Eugene C. Hunt, "Nell Houston Chisolm Quilt Top," *The Avery Research Center for African American History and Culture*, (Charleston, S. C. : College of Charleston, 1988), manuscript.
13. Lacy Folmar Bullard and Betty Jo Shiell, *Chintz Quilts: Unfading Glory* (Tallahassee, Florida: Serendipity Pub., 1983), *passim*; Laurel Horton and Lynn Robertson Myers, *Social Fabric: South Carolina's Traditional Quilts*, (Columbia, S. C.: The University of South Carolina, McKissick Museum, n.d.), pp. 11-18.
14. *Quilts: A Selection from the National Collection*, (Washington, D. C.: National Museum of American History, Smithsonian Institution, 1991), exhibition catalogue.

Chapter 3: Beyond Our Borders

During the nineteenth century African-Americans were among those responsible for the proliferation of American style quiltmaking beyond the borders of the United States. Via the Underground Railroad, many hundreds of escaped slaves settled in western Ontario, Canada. Arriving in Canada in a state of near destitution, they often encountered enormous difficulties, including hostile racist attitudes. Consequently, some of the black emigrés re-entered the United States. Until recently, the story of how black pioneers survived in Canada, established families, homes, churches, and became acculturated to their new land, has been obscure.[1] Initial research has already revealed that blacks made quilts in Canada, adhering to quiltmaking principles learned in their previous homes in the American South.

The introduction to Africa of traditional American quiltmaking is a singular example of the dissemination of the craft by African-Americans. An abolitionist organization, the American Colonization Society, had as its primary objective the repatriation of slaves to West Africa, to Sierre Leone and Liberia. Other abolitionist groups such as the American Anti-Slavery Society, the Female Anti-Slavery Society and the state Vigilance Committees posed strenuous objections to the American Colonization Society's policies. They declared it morally reprehensible to purchase blacks from slaveholders, thus rewarding them for their participation in the despicable practice of human trafficking. Further protests were made that blacks would be exiled to a land about which they had no knowledge because Africa was not a personal, remembered experience for many of the enslaved. Countless slaves were born in the United States and were several generations removed from their original African ancestors, kidnapped earlier and brought to America. Nevertheless, the American Colonization Society proceeded with its plans. In 1822, the first group of former slaves arrived at Providence Island, Liberia, aboard the ship *Nautilus*. Paul Boorstin wrote:

> *The Old World of repression that these immigrants — Pilgrims in reverse — fled was the United States of America. They called themselves Americo-Liberians and were essentially Americans, born and reared, with America's language, social ideas and stern Protestant religion. They had little sense of their original African roots, and no first hand experience of life in the tropics.*[2]

The former slaves transferred to Liberia the mores and customs of ante-bellum America. They christened their capital Monrovia to honor United States President James Monroe, and they adopted a flag design similar to that of the American flag. They further replicated the American experience by becoming the dominant political force, ruling the indigenous African population (just as had the Europeans earlier subjugated the native Americans in America). Some of Liberia's earliest settlers from the United States were identified as seamstresses, and those women are credited with the introduction of quiltmaking into Liberia.[3]

According to local Liberian lore, " . . . in the 1870's one Martha Ricks from Clay-Ashland stitched a quilt and presented it to Queen Victoria herself." By researching Martha Ricks' quilt, I was able to change its status from local lore to historical fact. Martha Ann Ricks, a former slave from Virginia, made a coffee tree quilt that she earnestly desired to give to the most noted woman of her time, the Queen of Great Britain, Empress of all India, Victoria Regina. Queen Victoria was held in high esteem by the Americo-Liberians because Great Britain, one year after Liberia declared its independence in 1847, was the first nation to recognize the fledgling republic as a free and sovereign country. The United States did not recognize Liberia's independence until 1862.

After years of waiting, Martha Ann Ricks, age 76, was granted the opportunity to travel by ship to London for an audience at Windsor Castle with Queen Victoria. Martha Ann Ricks was accompanied on the journey by Jane Roberts, wife of the first black president of Liberia, Joseph Jenkins Roberts.[4] On July 16, 1892, Martha Ann Ricks was presented to Queen Victoria, who graciously accepted the coffee tree quilt.[5] No records indicate that Martha Ann Ricks ever returned to America, but her quilt was exhibited in the United States. Queen Victoria sent the Martha Ann Ricks quilt in Her Majesty's British Needlework contingent to the World's Columbian Exposition, the Chicago World's Fair, in 1893.

Americo-Liberians have continued to make quilts until the present. Surprisingly, their quilts exhibit minimal influences of West African design traditions despite the Americo-Liberians' long residence in Liberia, and their intermarriages with native people. Liberian quilts retained essentially Americanized designs. Favored quilt patterns of Liberian quilts are "Bed of Roses," "Basket of Flowers," the "Liberian Star," the "Liberian Flag" and a log cabin type quilt called "Courthouse Steps" in the United States but in Liberia was titled "Columns" in Bensonville and "Solomon's Pillar" in Arthington. Prior to the recent disastrous civil war in Liberia, there had been an encouraging development in quiltmaking. At several locations, the Millsburg-Arthington-Clay-Ashland area, the Bensonville-Careysburg area, and in Greenville, small quilt cottage industries were formed to make quilts for sale. Quilting cooperatives in Liberia were given a modest grant by the U. S. Ambassador's Self-Help Fund.

> *The grant money was used by the women to purchase fabrics, notions, furniture and equipment that were needed for the cooperatives newly-acquired lodging. The group had previously been gathering on porches and balconies of neighbors' homes. . . The cooperative worked diligently for four months, and in March 1988, all their handiworks were displayed at the Monrovia City Hall. The event was an unqualified success: most of the quilts were sold and the women took orders to produce 17 more.* [6]

Two generations of an African-American family of missionaries were given quilts of honor by the Liberians. James Edward East, an African-American missionary for the National Baptist Convention of the United States of America, Inc. spent many years in Africa. Four of his children were born in South Africa during his eleven-year sojourn there. As Executive Secretary of the Foreign Mission Board, he traveled to Liberia and was presented with a quilt. The four block quilt (Figure #6) has a large dark red appliqued pineapple design in a style reminiscent of mid-nineteenth century American quilts, although his quilt was made in 1922. His daughter, Gladys East, after finishing college in the United States, also became a missionary. She spent many years in Liberia; and when she retired in 1986, she, too, was given a quilt by the Liberians — one in the appliqued "Bed of Roses" design.

Betsey Stockton, born in 1798, a freed former slave, served as a domestic in the home of the Rev. Dr. Green, president of Princeton College, New Jersey. Betsey Stockton was given unlimited access to the Green's large library and educated herself. She applied to the American Board of Commissioners of Foreign Missions to serve as a teacher, and her credentials were accepted. In 1822 she sailed with a group of missionaries aboard the ship "Thames" to the Sandwich Islands, arriving at Honolulu on April 27, 1823. The lush beauty of the islands amazed her.

> *On further acquaintance with Lahaina, B. Stockton remarked, that though it had been compared to Eden, she thought it more like the land "East of Eden."* [7]

Stockton was stationed at Lahaina, her mission assignment to conduct a school for "makaainana" or farmers and their wives and children. There is documentation that Betsey Stockton had a quilt; and while she may have taught quiltmaking to Hawaiians, no extant record has been found that she did so. Stella Jones, whose 1931 seminal study of Hawaiian quilts has been highly praised, wrote:

> No direct mention of quiltmaking is made in the records of these women [American missionary teachers], but it is reasonable to expect that little Hawaiian girls were given bits of cloth for piecework following the New England custom under which their instructors were reared.
>
> . . . A letter sent from the Sandwich Islands Mission to Boston in 1822 recounted, "We received from the Board by this conveyance (the schooner Rover) a box . . . and, with the rest, a bedquilt, for Kaahumana, which was very acceptable to the honored female ruler." [8]

There is an account of a group prayer meeting with Kaahumana, which Betsey Stockton attended. [9] It is a matter of record that Stockton, under the auspices of the American Mission Board conducted a school for Hawaiians. That the school was commended for its proficiency, and that she had a quilt, are also matters of record.[10] Additional research is required to determine if Betsey Stockton was one of those African-Americans who, during this early period, helped to spread the American style of quiltmaking beyond the borders of the United States.

1. Daniel G. Hill, *The Freedom Seekers: Blacks in Early Canada*, (Agincourt, Canada: The Book Society of Canada Limited, 1981).
   Jason Silverman, "Mary Ann Shadd and the Search for Equality," *Black Leaders in the Nineteenth Century*, ed. Leon Litwack and August Meier, (Urbana: University of Illinois Press, 1988), pp. 87-100.
2. Paul Boorstin, "Liberia's Fading Echoes of the Old American South," *Smithsonian Magazine*, (March 1976), p. 82.
3. Kathleen Bishop, "Quiltmakers of Liberia," *Topic: U. S. I. A. Magazine*, (Summer 1988), p. 47. Magazine circulated by the United States Information Agency solely to Africa. The law prohibits its circulation in the United States.
4. Hallie Q. Brown, *Homespun Heroines and Other Women of Distinction*, (Xenia, Ohio: Aldine Pub. Co., 1926), p. 47.
5. Cuesta Benberry, "A Quilt for Queen Victoria," *Quilter's Newsletter Magazine*, (February 1987), pp. 24-25.
6. Bishop, p. 48.
7. Hiram Bingham, A. M., *A Residence of Twenty-One Years in the Sandwich Islands*, (Rutland, Vermont: Charles E. Tuttle Co., 1847), p. 191.
8. Stella Jones, *Hawaiian Quilts*, (Honolulu: Honolulu Academy of Arts, 1930, p. 9; Reprint Ed., Honolulu: Daughters of Hawaii, 1973).
9. Bingham, p. 249.
10. *Missionary Album: Portraits and Biographical Sketches of the American Protestant Missionaries to the Hawaiian Islands*, (Honolulu, Hawaii: Hawaii Mission Children's Society, 1969; Enlarged from the Edition of 1937), pp. 186-187.

Chapter 4:
Post-Bellum Period: Elizabeth Keckley

Occasional confusion has arisen when post-bellum African-American quilts were classified as slave-made because the makers had once been enslaved. Even quilts of twentieth century origin have been called slave-made. A quilt cannot accurately be termed slave-made if it were made after the quiltmaker's emancipation.

Early in the post-bellum period, Elizabeth Hobbs Keckley made a densely embroidered silk hexagon patterned quilt with the word "Liberty" inscribed in its center medallion. (Figure #7) The quilt, circa 1870, was reportedly made from scraps of gowns created for Mary Todd Lincoln, wife of President Abraham Lincoln.[1] Elizabeth Keckley did preserve fabric pieces from Mary Todd Lincoln's gowns; several of those pieces were later donated to the archives at Wilberforce University in Ohio.[2]

Elizabeth Hobbs Keckley was born in Virginia in 1818 to slaves Agnes and George Pleasant Hobbs, who lived on different plantations. Agnes Hobbs, a seamstress in the Burwell household, taught her only child, Elizabeth, to sew. Elizabeth became an expert seamstress and a nursemaid for her master's children. Her agonizing youthful experiences refute a prevailing belief that house slaves enjoyed an idyllic existence compared to field slaves. When Elizabeth's owners, Anne Burwell Garland and Mr. Garland, experienced dire economic straits and moved to St. Louis, the decision was made to hire out the aged Agnes Hobbs. Elizabeth protested and persuaded the Garlands to allow her to sell her sewing services to prominent St. Louis families. She reported, "The best ladies in St. Louis were my patrons. . . With my needle I kept bread in the mouths of seventeen persons [her owners, their family, other slaves] for two years and five months."[3] "Elizabeth soon became active in the First African Baptist Church, where under the guise of a sewing class, she taught children to read and write and assisted John Berry Meachum in giving aid to blacks."[4] In 1855, with some assistance from her St. Louis clientele and the Anti-Slavery Society in New York, she purchased her freedom and that of her son George for twelve hundred dollars. Elizabeth Keckley moved to Washington, D. C., and became a leading modiste, serving the wives of Senator Jefferson Davis, Senator Stephen A. Douglas and Secretary Stanton. Eventually, she became the dressmaker and confidante of Mary Todd Lincoln.

In 1862 Keckley organized the Contraband Relief Association, "a society of colored people formed to labor for the benefit of unfortunate freedmen," and served as president of the organization for several years. When blacks were allowed to join the Union army, Keckley traveled extensively on behalf of the Contraband Relief Association, later retitled the Freedmen and Soldiers' Relief Association of Washington. She initiated fundraising activities and enlisted the aid of prominent black abolitionists such as Wendell Phillips, Frederick Douglass, Henry Highland Garnet and Sojouner Truth. President and Mrs. Lincoln contributed frequently to the Contraband Relief Association.[5] The Lincolns, notwithstanding their generous support of Mme. Keckley's organization, were creatures of their time, influenced by their upbringings and the social strictures of nineteenth century America. Elizabeth Keckley arranged for Sojourner Truth, the famous abolitionist orator and a great admirer of President Lincoln, to have an interview with the President. When Sojourner Truth, her grandson, Sammie, and her white friend, Lucy Coleman, were ushered into the President's office, Truth praised him as the Great Emancipator. Lucy Coleman later recorded the event.

> *Mr. Lincoln was not himself with this colored woman, he had no funny story for her, he called her aunty, as he would his washer woman, and when she complimented him as the first Anti-slavery President, he said, "I am not an Abolitionist; I wouldn't free the slaves if I could save the Union any other way. I am obliged to do it.*[6]

Lucy Coleman quickly ended the interview. She wrote, "We are not sure what Sojourner thought or said; for the first time in her life, she was speechless."[7]

After the assassination of President Lincoln, Mary Todd Lincoln, in distressing pecuniary difficulties, sent Elizabeth Keckley on a secret mission to New York to sell the elaborate Lincoln wardrobe. A scandal resulted when newspapers published the story of the proposed transaction, and Mrs. Lincoln was vilified. Hearing of the destitute condition of the wife of the President they so admired, black people rallied to her cause. H. H. Garnet and Frederick Douglass offered to embark on a fundraising lecture tour, all monies raised to be contributed to a fund established for Mary Lincoln. Elizabeth Keckley wrote:

> *I wrote to Mrs. Lincoln what we proposed to do, and she promptly replied, declining to receive aid from the colored people. I showed her letter to Mr. Garnet and Mr. Douglass, and the whole project was at once abandoned.*[8]

The book *Behind the Scenes: Thirty Years A Slave, Four Years in the White House* was written by Elizabeth Keckley to raise money for Mary Lincoln. When published, the book contained in the Appendix unedited letters written by Mary Lincoln to Elizabeth Keckley. Robert Lincoln was offended at the exposure of his mother's intimate thoughts and comments and enlisted the aid of his powerful friends to have the book suppressed. The friendship between Mary Todd Lincoln and Elizabeth Keckley came to an end.

In later years Elizabeth Keckley taught Domestic Science at Wilberforce University, the school her son George attended prior to enlisting in the Union army. Keckley's students' works were displayed in the Liberal Arts Building at the World's Columbian Exposition, the Chicago World's Fair, in 1893.[9] Elizabeth Keckley spent her last years in virtual obscurity in Washington, D. C., at the Home for Destitute Women and Children, an institution she had worked to organize during the war years. Her only source of income was a small a pension paid her as a survivor of her son who was killed in Missouri during the Civil War. Elizabeth Keckley died in 1907.[10]

1. Jennifer Lane, "The Quilt that Mrs. Keckley Made," *Ohio Antiques Review*, (February 1981), p. 23.
2. Monroe A. Majors, *Noted Negro Women: Their Triumphs and Activities*, (Chicago: Donohue and Henneberry, 1893), p. 260.
3. Elizabeth Keckley, *Behind the Scenes: Thirty Years A Slave, And Four Years in the White House*, (New York: New York Printing C., 1868; Reprint Ed., New York: Arno Press, 1968), p. 45.
4. John A. Wright, *No Crystal Stair: The Story of Thirteen Afro-Americans Who Once Called St. Louis Home*, (St. Louis, Mo.: Ferguson-Florissant District, 1988), p. 27.
5. Keckley, p. 114.
6. Dorothy Sterling, ed., *We Are Your Sisters: Black Women in the Nineteenth Century*, (New York: W. W. Norton, 1984), p. 252.
7. Jeanne Noble, *Beautiful, Also, Are the Souls of My Black Sisters: A History of the Black Woman in America*, (Englewood Cliffs, N. J.: Prentice-Hall, 1978), p. 55.
8. Keckley, p. 314.
9. Majors, p. 260.
10. Wright, p. 29.

Chapter 5: Bible Quilts

Early research of African-American post-bellum and twentieth century quilts supports the theory that the making of Bible quilts was idiosyncratic to southern black women. Two late nineteenth century machine appliqued Bible quilts made by Harriet Powers, Athens, Georgia, a former slave, have as their motifs incidents from the Holy Scriptures and depictions of unique physical phenomena. Unable to read and write, Powers recorded legends she had heard on her quilts, continuing an African oral tradition in which stories customarily taught lessons, recorded historical events, reinforced values, imparted religious beliefs, instructed in survival techniques and entertained. Harriet Powers' narrative quilts are thus creative transmutations of oral imagery to visual imagery on cloth. Striking parallels between the design motifs on the Powers' quilts and the appliqued banner designs of the Fon people of Dahomey [Benin] have been noted.[1] Brilliant animal and figural appliques of the Fon decorated banners, flags, state umbrellas, hammocks, pavilions and ceremonial caps and were made exclusively by restricted guilds commissioned by royalty to do the work. Symbolic in nature, the vivid appliques represented battles and heraldic devices, illustrated proverbs and transmitted subtle messages. Dating back to the seventeenth century or earlier, the African symbolic motifs were appliqued to raffia cloth and subsequently to European trade cloth when, circa 1890, it became available in Dahomey. The resemblance between the motifs of the Powers' quilts, especially the animals, and those of the Dahomey banners, is striking.

Harriet Powers' Bible quilts are housed in the National Museum of American History, Smithsonian Institution, Washington, D. C., and in the Museum of Fine Arts, Boston. The peculiar dimensions of the Powers' quilt in the Boston Museum collection is a cause for speculation among quilt scholars. That quilt is much wider (105 1/4 inches) than it is long (67 1/8 inches), very curious proportions for a bedcover that can be placed, because of its design, on a bed in one direction only. The Powers Bible quilt was commissioned by the wives of Atlanta University professors and given to Reverend Charles Cuthbert Hall, then Chairman of the Board of Trustees, in 1898.[2] Questions to ponder about the Harriet Powers Bible quilt: Why was the quilt made in this odd shape? Is it possible that this Bible quilt was designed to be hung on the wall rather than put on a bed?

Evidence of the strength of an oral tradition within the African-American experience is notably visible in the Bible quilts. Imaginations were more electrified by the soul-stirring sermons of African-American preachers than the widely distributed, illustrated

Sunday School lesson cards and religious literature that depicted all Biblical characters as white people. An original African-American "Bible Scenes" quilt, circa 1900, was handed down in the Drake family of Thomaston, Georgia. (Figure #8) It is a four block quilt; but only two Bible scenes, "Adam and Eve" and "The Crucifixion," are shown. In years past, many African-American preachers would deliver emotion-laden sermons and exclaim the phrase, "The Alpha and the Omega, the Beginning and the End!" Not content always to quote unchanged the Biblical statement that God was the Beginning and the End, some ministers would give the words new meanings. Additionally, they would refer to Adam and Eve as the Beginning and to Jesus Christ's Crucifixion as the End (meaning not the end of the world, but the climaxing epoch of the Faith).

In each of the two nearly identical Adam and Eve squares of the "Bible Scenes" quilt, a huge serpent is wrapped around a tree in a fenced Garden of Eden. The serpent's head is quite close to Eve, as if it were speaking to her. However, the two "Crucifixion" squares are not identical. On the upper block, "Jesus Christ on the Cross" is the dominant figure; and placed sideways, to minimize the impact, is one of the thieves' crosses, slightly aslant, being prepared for erection. On the lower "Crucifixion" block, Jesus Christ's dominance is indicated by his slightly larger cross. Jesus Christ, the two thieves, Adam and Eve are all dark figures; other figures, perhaps Roman soldiers, are either dark or red.

Strategically placed on the quilt top are appliqued letters J, C, H, L, A, E, G, T and such designs as an axe-like object and what appears to be two ladders. As the letters A, E, and G are affixed only to the "Adam and Eve" squares, it is likely the A meant Adam and E was for Eve. The letter G is placed at the opening of the fenced in Garden of Eden, so G probably meant Garden of Eden. The G is also a symbol used by the Free Masonry Orders. On the "Crucifixion" blocks, J and C are located near the top of the Cross and evidently were meant to identify Jesus Christ. Other symbolisms on the quilt squares are more mystifying. For instance, did the axe, the ladders, a T-square-like object relate to Jesus Christ's vocation as a carpenter; or were they instruments of the Passion or possibly emblematic images from fraternal societies? Much of the iconography of the "Bible Scenes" quilt remains shrouded and mysterious.

When enigmatic symbols are encountered on early African-American quilts, a current tendency is to attribute them to an unconscious African cultural memory on the part of the quiltmaker. Nevertheless, this is only one of a number of avenues to explore. Perhaps the decision to apply symbols to her quilt was a conscious, deliberate act of the quiltmaker, inspired by something more immediate in her environment. Various black fraternal orders, lodges and benevolent associations, such as the Masonic lodges, the Odd Fellows, the Knights of Tabor and the Elks, played a key role in the lives of numerous African-American families from the post-bellum era into the twentieth century. Options were limited for African-Americans to obtain insurance from commercial carriers. White-owned insurance companies refused to write policies on black people, citing their lower life expectancy.[3] Blacks turned frequently to their fraternal organizations to obtain what small sickness and accident stipends and death benefits they could. Other benefits were ceremonial rites of honor at funerals and the opportunity for social interaction. Nearly all of the organizations had secret symbols that identified them, were known to the members, and may have appeared on their quilts. Additionally, there are many sources of information, as yet uninvestigated, about the daily lives of African-Americans. Research is required to disclose the environmental factors which influenced African-American quiltmaking.

A black washerwoman's experience in making a Bible quilt on a southern plantation is related in a non-fiction article written in 1922. With great joy, the washerwoman described the quilt blocks she made successfully. Her inability to make the blocks "Daniel in the lion's den," and "the three Hebrew children in the fiery furnace" was a source of irritation to the proud quiltmaker. Her Bible quilt was her most prized creation. She said, "I got a log cabin quilt an' a sunrisin' quilt, but my Bible quilt tecks de shine off dem."[4]

Julia Peterkin, a close observer of southern black plantation life, wrote a fictionalized account of a quilting party in her novel, *Black April*. The party's star attraction was Maum Hannah, an elderly black woman, who displayed and told the stories on her twenty-block Bible quilt. "Many eyes in the room glistened with tears."[5]

Continuation of the vitality of the religious narrative tradition in African-American life is demonstrated in the late twentieth century quilt creations of artists such as Yvonne Wells, Tuscaloosa; Peggie Hartwell, New York; Anita Holman Knox, Houston; Viola Canady, Washington, D. C.; and Lorraine Mahan, Philadelphia. Lorraine Mahan, born in Ocean City, New Jersey, reared in Philadelphia, has been making quilts in original designs for nearly thirty years. Although taught quiltmaking by her grandmother, who reared her, Lorraine Mahan is quick to point out that her quilts are unlike her grandmother's. Mrs. Mahan's quilts are appliqued; her grandmother's quilts were pieced. Beautiful drawings done in Mahan's childhood gave evidence of her artistic talent. Lorraine Mahan used appliqued pictures and cut out letters when she began to make quilts. A number of them are "message documents" that required the making of cut-out letters. Utilizing a system devised over many years of practice, she cuts the letters (often as small as 1/2 inch), free hand, without using a template. Her appliqued message quilts range from the small wall hanging, "Four Gems of the Bible," containing the "Beatitudes," the "Lord's Prayer," the "Ten Commandments," and the "23rd Psalm," to the full-sized quilt, "Old and New Testament Quilt," with its appliqued Bible verses, to an oversized quilt with the complete "119th Psalm."

Lorraine Mahan's Bible quilt of 1974, centered with a lettered "The Lord's Prayer" surrounded by such graphic blocks as "Noah and the Ark," "Moses and the Burning Bush," "David and Goliath," and "Samson in the Temple," is a combination of her favorite modalities, pictorial depictions and lettered messages. (Figure #9) Mrs. Mahan has made quilts that necessitated considerable research such as the "Jewish Quilt" which incorporated various symbolic Judaic references. When she gave the quilt to a Jewish friend, she was gratified to be told each symbol she used was accurate and appropriate. Although Mrs. Mahan has fabricated numerous quilts with Judaeo-Christian themes, not all of her quilts illustrated religious topics. Another research-based quilt is her "Indian Healing Quilt," composed of American Indian "Zodiac" designs. Instead of employing the familiar astrological symbols of the zodiac, Mahan followed the Indian practice of representing the months with animal and flowers. For accuracy she researched her "Indian Healing Quilt" but she was not working on a subject personally unfamiliar to her. She has kinship ties with Native Americans because she, like many black people in America, has a mixed African, Native American and white heritage. Lorraine Mahan gives her quilts to relatives, friends, and persons she admires, such as President Jimmy Carter and Mayor Wilson Goode of Philadelphia.[6] She has never sold one.

1. John Michael Vlach, *The Afro-American Tradition in Decorative Arts*, (Cleveland, Ohio: Cleveland Museum of Art, 1978), pp. 43-67.
2. *A Pattern Book, Based on an Applique Quilt by Mrs. Harriet Powers, American, 19th Century*, (Boston: Museum of Fine Arts, n. d.), p. 00.
3. Dwight W. Hoover, *The Red and the Black*, (Chicago: Rand McNally College Pub., 1976), p. 166.
4. Eleanor C. Gibbs, "The Bible Quilt," *Atlantic Monthly*, (July 1922), pp. 65-66.
5. Julia Peterkin, *Black April*, (Bobbs-Merrill, 1927), pp. 159-179.
6. Taped interview of Lorraine Mahan by author, 19 May 1991.

Chapter 6: Late Nineteenth Century

By the late post-bellum era, some African-American quiltmakers were participating in the various quilt fads sweeping the country; the making of crazy quilts, charm quilts, pieced silk quilts, outline embroidery quilts and realistic quilts. Ruth Finley stated in a chapter entitled "The Decline of Handicraft":

> *...for what might be called realistic quilts there was a veritable craze, beginning about 1870....Women cut in silhouette every shape imaginable, to be appliquéd as quilt patches. And many of the results, such as "The Old Town Pump" were grotesque in the extreme.*

A nineteenth century African-American silhouette quilt that conforms partially to Finley's description is the "Lady's Shoe" quilt made by Fanny Cork, Grand Rivers, Kentucky. Fanny Cork's design replicates in silhouette the high top shoes worn by women of her time. Yet, the Cork quilt does not comply completely with Finley's criteria. While at first glance the quilt may appear to be appliqued, it is not. "Lady's Shoe" is a pieced quilt; and it was made, circa 1890, twenty years after the fad purportedly began. Cork obviously cut her shoe designs "by eye" rather than using a template because all of the shoes are not the same size, and they vary in other details as well.

Fanny Catlett was born in 1859 in Birmingham, Kentucky. She married Jack Cork, and they became farmers after moving to Grand Rivers, Kentucky. Fanny Cork, a prolific quilter, taught each of her four pretty daughters to make quilts. (The daughters were so pretty, people in the area made up a pun about them, "Those Cork girls are real stoppers!") Fanny Cork cherished her "Lady's Shoe" quilt. Despite all of the quilts she made, "Lady's Shoe" is her only known surviving quilt. (Figure #10)

Black women's works were entered in the late post-bellum period's major cultural event, the World's Columbian Exposition, the Chicago World's Fair of 1893. A *New York Times*, June 10, 1893, article "Work of Colored Women" stated:

> *Hand-made lace, crochet and hairpin lace, and modern guipre and point Duchesse lace, and very fine and delicate scarfings are the handiwork of a colored woman. Very good oil and color paintings, Mexican drawn work, ecclesiastical embroidery, decorative work in china, quilting, etc. are given a conspicuous position . . .*

Susie King Taylor, an African-American, whose reminiscences of life in camp during the Civil War with the 33rd U. S. Colored Troops, late 1st South Carolina Volunteers, were published in 1902, was a remarkable woman. (A recent film "Glory" detailed the exploits of those black soldiers.) In 1886, she helped to organize Massachusetts Corps 67, Women's Relief Corps, an auxiliary to the Grand Army of the Republic (G. A. R.), the Union Army's veteran's organization. Susie King Taylor reported about a quilt she made:

> In 1898 the Department of Mass. W. R. C. [Women's Relief Corps] gave a grand fair at Music Hall. I made a large quilt of red, white and blue ribbon that made quite a sensation. The quilt was voted for and was awarded to the Department President, Mrs. E. L. W. Waterman, of Boston.[2]

A turn of the century, circa 1900, dark blue and white cotton appliqued *"Fleur de Lis"* quilt was made in a family of black Creoles, or as they were historically termed, Creoles of color. In Louisiana and the Gulf States, interracial descendants of French and African parentage formed a large and distinct ethnic group.

> In New Orleans, as well as in other parts of the Gulf region that were long under Spanish and French control, there existed by the mid-nineteenth century sizeable and significant group known as the gens de couleur libre . . . [they] . . . were colored Creoles, a racially mixed group whose numbers had been augmented by West Indian emigrés fleeing the instability of the Haitian Revolution in the eighteenth and early nineteenth centuries and by French Creoles expelled from Cuba in 1809.[3]

Prior to the Civil War, the racially mixed Creoles of color, very often free persons, comprised the middle group of a Louisiana regional three-tier caste system, consisting of white people, colored Creoles, and enslaved blacks. Although Creoles of color were partially African, they identified more with the French than with the blacks. They spoke the French language, practiced the Catholic religion, and were oriented toward the French culture. Many of the wealthy colored Creoles sent their children to France to be educated. As with most southerners, the Civil War and its aftermath wrought severe dislocations in the lives of Creoles of color. They were no longer accorded a special caste designation in the society. After the imposition of Jim Crow laws, the disenfranchisement of blacks through the "grandfather clause" and other harsh anti-black measures, both legal and illegal, there was a slow movement toward unity between the Creoles of color and the emancipated blacks.

Sara Miller, a Creole from whose family came the *"Fleur de Lis"* quilt, lived in Natchez, Mississippi. *"Fleur de Lis,"* a medallion quilt, contains four dark blue *flower of lily* motifs at its center, surrounded by two border-like formations of the designs, all framed within a straight strip border of dark blue. A wide white border completes the quilt. (Figure 11) The quilt, a cherished family heirloom, was given to Portia Robb Higgins by her grandmother, Magdalene Miller, the late Sara Miller's sister-in-law.

1. Ruth Finley, *Old Patchwork Quilts and The Women Who Made Them,* (Philadelphia: J. P. Lippincott, 1929), p. 194.
2. Susie King Taylor, *Reminiscences of My Life in Camp with the 33rd U. S. Colored Troops, Late 1st South Carolina Volunteers,* (Boston: Self-published, 1902); Reprint Ed., *Susie King Taylor: A Black Woman's Civil War Memoirs,* (New York: Markus Wiener Pub., 1988). Collection of Virginia Gunn.
3. Willard B. Gatewood, *Aristocrats of Color: The Black Elite, 1880-1920,* (Bloomington: Indiana University Press, 1990), pp. 82, 83.

Chapter 7: Perkins Family Quilts

An extraordinary collection of African-American quilts of unquestioned historicity is the Perkins' family quilts. Made by several generations in a single family, from the late nineteenth century to mid-twentieth century, the documented quilts were most often original to the makers and remain today in an unaltered state. The quilts were made in both urban and rural

settings by a middle class African-American family and represent a quiltmaking continuum. Fabrics utilized were silks, rayons, wools, printed and plain cottons. All of the quilts except one were meant to serve as bedcovers, and they range from basic utilitarian covers to purposely decorative show pieces. As we had access to quilts made by several generations in a family, we did not have to follow the usual practice of displaying a single quilt as a typical example of an African-American family's quilts. A discrete analysis of these quilts within the context of the family's chronicles, allowed a balanced view of them to be formed, with equal weight given matters of iconography, the pragmatic concerns of the makers (the purposes for which the quilts were made, for instance), their differing skill levels, and regional and environmental influences.

Marshall L. Perkins, (1846-1912), Trevilians, Virginia, husband of Mima Thompson Perkins, father of their eight children, a prosperous farmer and a minister. Marshall Perkins gave strong support to his family of "quilting women." Photograph in the collection of the Perkins-Wilbourn family.

The Perkins family quilt annals begin with Mima Thompson Perkins, the quiltmaking matriarch. Mima Thompson was born on December 31, 1847, in Trevilians, Louisa County, in North Central Virginia near Charlottesville. When Mima Thompson, the daughter of a preacher, married Marshall L. Perkins, a minister, on August 26, 1869, in Trevilians, she was twenty-one years of age. She possessed the necessary skills to be an excellent homemaker, as she and Marshall managed their homestead that consisted of a large house and many acres of farmland. On their farm, they raised crops of corn, wheat, hay and cultivated large gardens. Eight children were born to Marshall and Emma Perkins, four sons and four daughters. Their children were reared in a loving atmosphere, were taught to value education highly, and were raised to be self-reliant and self-sufficient. Both sons and daughters were taught to cook, sew, and to do household chores without a gender identification being attached to any domestic task.

A favorite recreation for the family was playing croquet on any level surface they could find. One son, James, was a proficient whittler,

51

and he hand-carved croquet mallets for the family's games. A number of the children (family oral history said all eight) attended Virginia State College (now Virginia State University) in Petersburg, and at least three graduated, Lloyd and Cordelia in 1902 and Roscoe in 1912. Lloyd, the eldest, became the third generation minister in the family. Cordelia, the oldest daughter, was a nurse and a teacher; Emma, the youngest daughter, also became a teacher. Roscoe became a dentist and moved to Ohio. James was a farmer, who maintained the family farm until his death.

Mima Perkins, an expert quiltmaker, taught her daughters to quilt. However, only Eva and Emma practiced quiltmaking to a great extent, with Emma becoming the more skilled quilter of the two. Eva's greater talent for cooking became legendary in family lore. Emma, being the youngest, benefited from having more time with her mother to

practice the art of quiltmaking while her older siblings were away at school. Mima Perkins and Emma would cut quilt patches, then spread them out on the floor, adjusting and re-adjusting the patches to form a pattern and finding color placements pleasing to them. Seemingly there was no scarcity of materials for quiltmaking, as the Perkins' stores of fabrics were often replenished by fabric exchanges with neighbors, the exchanges usually taking place on Sundays at the local church. What a happy time it was for the Perkins family when, as family history relates, relatives came from afar to visit, bringing their latest quilt to be exclaimed over, sharing new quilt designs, and exchanging many fabric scraps that had been saved for just this occasion.

Emma Perkins moved to Mt. Hope, West Virginia, to teach in a one-room school. Her brother Lloyd's wife, Jessie, was a principal of a school in Williamson, West Virginia. Emma Perkins met and married George Wilbourn, a coal miner, and two children, George and Vera, were born to the couple. When George Wilbourn, Sr., was injured in a coal mine accident in 1926, the family moved to Philadelphia; and after a year or so, the Wilbourns relocated to New York City at the insistence of Emma's sister, Cordelia. Moving to New York never strained the ties of this close-knit family, as Emma Perkins Wilbourn and her family returned regularly to the home place in Trevilians for visits. Every year, Emma sent her children, George and Vera, to Virginia to

The Perkins-Wilbourn Family Bible contains the records of the 25 August 1869 marriage of Mima Thompson and Marshall L. Perkins. The birthdates of the Perkins parents and of each of the eight children were also entered on the Bible pages. Collection of the Perkins-Wilbourn family.
(Bible photographs by Gene Gissin.)

spend their summer vacations with their grandparents. Emma and George Wilbourn did not believe New York was the best environment for children who had so much free time in the summer.

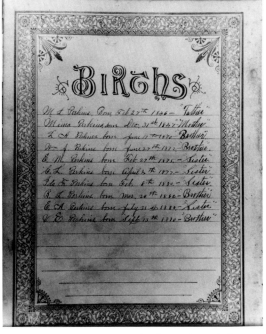

Emma Wilbourn continued to make quilts both with her mother during visits to Trevilians and less frequently in her New York home. Her inability to devote as much time to quiltmaking as she would have liked was a cause for some frustration. George Wilbourn reported his mother would exclaim, "Boy, it's been so long. I've got to work on my quilts!" From his description of his mother's quiltmaking activities, it appears Emma Wilbourn lap-quilted her bed covers.[1]

The oldest quilt in the Perkins-Wilbourn collection is a circa 1890 crazy quilt made by Mima Thompson Perkins. (Figure #12) Some crazy quilts of the more sophisticated variety had purchased design elements applied to them. (There was a thriving commercial market that supplied silk pieces and small ready-made designs to apply to crazy quilts.)[2] Mima Perkin's woolen crazy quilt, incorporating home-made design motifs, celebrated her family in a very personal manner. She commemorated the family's favorite pastime by placing croquet mallets on the quilt. The word "Hurrah," George Wilbourn believes, was meant to acknowledge the accomplishments of Mima Perkins' children. A small hand (a child's hand, no doubt), an embroidered house, a simplified tree (the number of tree branches possibly indicating the family members), as well as grouped initials (identified by George and Vera as family persons) reinforced the intimate qualities of the quilt. Mima Perkins' crazy quilt was constructed in a contained crazy quilt style with each block made separately and then sewn together to form the top. Most unusual, and unlike any other of the crazy squares, is a pieced block of rectangular patches at the center top row. Vera Wilbourn Holtzman, Mima Perkins granddaughter, reports that the out-of-context square was not inserted willy-nilly on the quilt but had special significance to the family. A lining of soft blues, reds, and browns in a cheater cloth pattern of "A Thousand Pyramids" completed the quilt.

A silk and wool parlor quilt in a variation of the strip pattern sewn with fancy stitches was made by Mima Perkins, circa 1890. The subdued colors of the quilt are enlivened by the sheen of the silk threads used for the embroidery stitches and by the red strips that frame the muted squares. That considerable care and planning went into the making of the parlor quilt can be discerned in the small pieced squares at each corner of the border and, within the body of the quilt, each half triangle was carefully pieced of two different fabrics. (Figure #13)

A charming quilt in the Perkins-Wilbourn collection is a rarely seen "buggy quilt." Family members recall riding in an open Model T car and covering up with the buggy quilt. At times, the buggy quilt would touch the wheels, and today oil stains on the quilt are reminders of those misadventures. Happy memories are associated with the buggy quilt as it was also used for cover when the family rode in horsedrawn sleds over the countryside. Pieced very casually and crudely, and presumably quickly quilted, the buggy quilt resembles an unadorned country crazy quilt. It is an excellent example of a quilt made for a specific utilitarian purpose because a quiltmaker's intentions have much to do with a quilt's construction. Mima Perkins made the buggy quilt in all of its rustic charm, and yet she is the same person who made the carefully planned parlor quilt. What may appear to be a paradox evidently presented no problem for Mima Perkins, who sensibly did not lavish the same care on a buggy quilt as she did on a quilt to be placed in her parlor. (Figure #14)

One of the most appealing quilts in the collection represents the traditional characteristics of softness, warmth, and simplicity of design so valued in early bed quilts. Made in soft woolen flannels, the completely hand-pieced quilt top in a "Brick Work" pattern, circa 1915, is attributed to Eva Perkins and because of its meticulous piecing was probably a joint project of Eva Perkins and Mima Perkins. A variety of soft, lightweight striped flannel materials was utilized; such fabrics were identified by quilt historian Barbara Brackman as shirting flannels that became popular in the first two decades of the twentieth century. Some of the striped rectangular "brick" patches were made from two pieces of fabric. Often the two pieces were sewn to form a chevron pattern within the rectangle and care was taken that the stripes met at the same angle, an exhibition of fastidiousness in a utilitarian quilt. Alternate placing of light and dark bricks framed by the wide,

Mima Thompson Perkins, (1847-1920), Trevilians, Virginia, who with her husband, Marshall L. Perkins, raised eight children. Mima Perkins, a prolific quiltmaker, taught her four daughters to make quilts. Some of the quilts of Mima Perkins and those of two of her daughters, Emma Perkins Wilbourn and Eva Perkins Ragsdale, are shown in the catalogue. (Figures 11 - 17) Photograph of Mima Perkins, circa 1900, from the collection of the Perkins-Wilbourn family.

orange-striped sashing resulted in a quilt top of uncommon beauty. (Figure #15)

Visually striking is the machine and hand-pieced cotton quilt top made by Emma Perkins Wilbourn, circa 1900-1925 in an unusual pattern, its name presently unknown. Triangles of half squares are

reminiscent of the "Wild Goose Chase" pattern, and the wedge-shaped designs seen at intervals could be the "Arrowhead" or "Fish" design. Yet the particular overall configuration of the top remains elusive as to a quilt name. Lavender and black check fabrics were used, but the color values are so close, no abrupt changes are obvious. It was frequently the task of the children in the Perkins-Wilbourn family to sort fabrics by color and place them in different storage boxes, making color selections for quilt patches more convenient for the adult quiltmakers. (Figure #16)

Emma Perkins Wilbourn, (1888-1986), and Eva Perkins Ragsdale, (1875-1986), sisters born in Trevilians, Virginia. Both daughters were taught quiltmaking by their mother, Mima Thompson Perkins. Photograph in the collection of the Perkins-Wilbourn family.

Another circa 1900-1925 cotton quilt in the Perkins-Wilbourn collection was pieced by Emma Perkins Wilbourn. (Figure #17) In attempting to assign a name to the quilt, we were advised by Barbara Brackman that the most common names, "Grandmother's Pride" and "The Queen's Favorite," were inappropriate. Those two names came from published commercial sources that did not date prior to 1925. The quilt pattern is a very old one, and the top was made in the first two decades of the twentieth century. So we are applying an earlier name, "The Album," to the quilt. "The Album" quilt blocks were strip sashed in red, the strips running in one direction only without any intersecting sashing. The incomplete "The Album" quilt gives evidence of being made in two stages; the top in the early part of the twentieth century — the batting added and the quilting begun late in Emma Perkins Wilbourn's life in her New York home. George Wilbourn remembers this quilt as one of the last ones on which his mother worked. Of great interest is the batting; an old blanket, not quite large enough, and added to this a folded, worn bath towel. The top, batting and lining are basted with white cord string; and one corner was crudely quilted. Sharp contrast exists between the skill-fully made top, constructed early in the century by Emma Wilbourn, and the quilting on it done much later in her life when advancing age affected the work of this, the most proficient quilter of Mima Perkin's children. Emma Perkins Wilbourn died in 1986 at the age of ninety-eight.

A simple, large, one-patch scrap quilt top (Figure #18) made by Eva Perkins Ragsdale, circa 1940, serves more as an album of fabrics available at the time of making than as an accomplished piece of work. Cotton chintzes (some of which may have been furnishings fabrics), cotton checks, stripes, plaids and several rayons went into the top. As the top was constructed after the death of Mima Perkins, Eva P. Ragsdale, never deemed by the family a fine quiltmaker, no longer had the guidance of her mother to produce a work of the quality of the "Brick Work" quilt made many years earlier.[3]

The Perkins family quilts were given a prominent place in this exhibition as they conclusively support my thesis that the historical record of African-American quiltmakers should be one of inclusion, not exclusion; that a definition of African-American quiltmakers which extracts from the entire group only those persons whose works conform to stated and implied criteria is unacceptable.

The Perkins family record reveals: a close-knit, multi-generational, middle-class African-American family which included quiltmakers; a family whose quiltmaking spans the nineteenth and twentieth centuries; family members whose quilts were made in both urban and rural settings; individual family members who varied their quiltmaking techniques according to the purposes intended for a specific quilt, resulting in marked contrasting levels of skill in works made by the same person; that natural processes, such as aging, can affect the quiltmaking abilities of some makers; and that a quilt's value to this family depended not on the competence of the quiltmaker but on the sentimental value of the work of a loved relative.

1. Taped interview of Vera Wilbourn Holtzman by Jonathan Holstein, 27 February 1991.
2. Penny McMorris, *Crazy Quilts*, (New York: E. P. Dutton, 1984), p. 20 ". . . there were pre-embroidered appliques which could be purchased and sewn onto crazy quilt patches." p. 19 ". . . perforated patterns."
3. Taped interview of George Wilbourn by Jonathan Holstein, 3 March 1991. (The Perkins family quilts were discovered by Jonathan Holstein. In addition to the formal taped interviews listed above, numerous informal conversations between the Wilbourn family members and Jonathan Holstein occurred, accompanied by extensive examinations of the quilts. The research for much of this important section of the exhibition was conducted by Jonathan Holstein with grateful appreciation from the author.)

Chapter 8: African-American Quilts in the Twentieth Century

With the advent of the twentieth century, two institutions remained paramount in the lives of the majority of African-Americans: the church and the school. The powerful religious beliefs that had sustained countless black people during the dark, perilous times of slavery could be openly practiced in formally organized, independent churches once Emancipation was in place, institutions blacks could truly call their own. In addition to providing a place for the free and uninhibited practise of religion, the role of the black church expanded. It became a means of fostering social reforms, a place where goals for the furtherance of education for blacks could be set and in some instances the church even provided political leadership. During the Reconstruction period, a number of church-sponsored colleges were established concurrently with the organization of state-sponsored land grant colleges for black people. African-Americans were steadfast in their belief that the education long denied them offered the primary means by which black people, and especially their children, would take their rightful place in American society. Blacks, wealthy and poor, contributed to their churches' educational and foreign missions programs. Blacks did not forget their brothers overseas, particularly in Africa, nor did they fail to remember their recent history and the heroes who emerged during those tragic times.

African-American commemorative quilts are a graphic means to determine the values placed by blacks on family, church, school and black history. A unique signature quilt of Emporia, Kansas, honors four black churches from four separate denominations. It is not unusual to find a signature quilt that memorializes a single church; it is indeed rare to find one that commemorates four churches of different denominations. On the quilt are listed the names of the churches, their pastors, and the churches' addresses: St. James Baptist Church, Rev. C. P. Morrow, 915 Commercial St.; Second Christian Church, Rev. B. C. Duke, 728 Congress St.; A. M. E. Church, Rev. T. J. Sanford, 601 Congress St. ["A. M. E."= African Methodist Episcopal Church]; C. M. E. Church, Rev. J. W. Jacobs, 814 East St. ["C. M. E."=Colored Methodist Episcopal Church, later Christian Methodist Episcopal Church]. Embroidered in turkey red thread, the quilt, dated 1916, is in the "Wheel" quilt pattern. Other church members' names are embroidered on the red border with a date of 1930. Much of the handwriting on the border is similar to the writing on the body of the quilt. The prevailing belief at present is that the quilt was made in 1930 as a memorial to the pastors and members who belonged to each church in 1916, and thus the quilt is a historical record of four black churches in Emporia, Kansas. The signature quilt came from the estate of

Ashley Washam. (Figure #19)

In the mid-twentieth century, two appliqued quilts honoring African-American historic figures, Harriet Tubman and Frederick Douglass, were made by the integrated Negro History Club of Marin City and Sausalito, California. Each quilt was designed by Benjamin Irvin and sewn by the club members. Both quilts were purchased by the Howard Thurman Educational Trust and later given as permanent donations to the Robert W. Woodruff Library, Atlanta University, Atlanta, Georgia, by Mrs. Sue Thurman.

The "Harriet Tubman" quilt (Figure #20), made in 1951, portrays the somber figure of Harriet "Moses" Tubman in the foreground; in the background are slaves she was leading to freedom via the Underground Railroad; an owl denotes her wisdom and ability to successfully travel at night; and in the dark sky, the North Star, used by Tubman as a guide, shines brightly. A fascinating pictorial depiction, the "Harriet Tubman" quilt won second place at the 1952 California State Fair; and it was later on display at the Harriet Tubman Home, now designated an historic site, in Auburn, New York.[1]

The second quilt made by the Negro History Club in 1953, the "Frederick Douglass" quilt, was somewhat more intricately detailed than the Tubman quilt. Known as an eloquent, spell-binding orator, Frederick Douglass is shown as a young man at his initial lecture, delivered to an American Anti-Slavery Society Convention audience in Nantucket, Massachusetts, in 1841. In his audience are his wife, to the left, and William Lloyd Garrison, the famous abolitionist editor, to the right. Two bunting-draped white columns frame the commanding figure of Frederick Douglass to complete the handsome quilt. Immediate fame came to the "Frederick Douglass" quilt when it received extensive coverage in numerous publications and was exhibited at a number of venues, including the 1972 *Patch In Time* quilt exhibition held in Mill Valley, California.[2] (Figure #21)

The meteoric rise to prominence of Frederick Douglass, an escaped slave, dedicated abolitionist, impassioned lecturer and editor, did not end with the issuance of the Emancipation Proclamation. Subsequently, Douglass became the United States Recorder of Deeds in Washington, D. C., and his final assignment was as Minister to Haiti. His last home sits atop a high hill in Washington, D. C., and is now a museum administered by the U. S. Parks Service. In the stately old home's bedrooms are several rather worn quilts, but it is doubtful that the quilts have any connection to the Douglass family. What is not doubtful is his connection to the 1880-1881 autograph album quilt he signed. The "Ohio Star"-patterned quilt is replete with autographs, some dated, of Presidents, famous politicians, renowned military men, leading literary persons, and other late nineteenth century celebrities. There among the many luminaries' signed blocks is one with the autograph, "Fred. Douglass."[3]

Much venerated for his intellectual prowess and intrepid spirit, Frederick Douglass became the African-Americans' symbol for human freedom. Throughout the nation, all-black institutions such as hospitals and schools were named for him. In a small Missouri town near St. Louis, Webster Groves, black children attended the Douglass Elementary School for many years. When the U. S. Supreme Court outlawed the "separate but equal doctrine," Webster Groves integrated its school system and closed the Douglass School. Years later, the interior of the Douglass School was completely gutted, and new apartments for senior people were built. Most of the apartment dwellers were Webster Groves residents and had attended the Douglass school when they were children. To keep the memory of the Douglass School alive, they made a Frederick Douglass School commemorative quilt, circa 1980, recording the names of its principals, state-wide honors the school had achieved, an Honor Roll of former graduates, the dates of its opening and closing, and a brief biography of Frederick Douglass. The memory quilt was hung in the beautiful atrium of the Douglass School Apartments building.[4]

An earlier African-American commemorative school quilt was made in the small town of Garland located in the northeastern county of Bowie, Texas. Garland, an all-black community three miles west of DeKalb, Texas, was named for the white owner of a large plantation who, after emancipation, subdivided his land and gave parcels of it to his former slaves. Black students attended the Garland High School from 1875 until it was closed in 1955 when the black schools were consolidated with the former all-white schools in the DeKalb school district. Prior to the time of the school's consolidation, the Garland High School commemorative quilt was made in 1948-1949. That season the Garland High School had an outstanding basketball team; and to honor the team the school's music teacher, Mrs. Lila A. Kelley (Brown), and the P. T. A. president, Mrs. Lizzie Shavers, made the quilt. Centered on the quilt is an appliqued map of Bowie County, and on the map is a three-dimensional head of a black bear, the team's mascot. The appliqued quilt is in pink and white with a scalloped border; pink and white were used, Mrs. Kelly-Brown reported, "because pink is my favorite color." Embroidered on the

quilt in black thread are the names of the school's trustees, superintendent, and some faculty members. Mrs. Lila A. Kelley (Brown) is listed as the quilt's designer; "quilted by the P. T. A." referred to Mrs. Kelley-Brown and Mrs. Shavers.[5] (Figure #22)

One of the most engaging examples of family quilting was related by Ernestine Hamer Bates, the daughter of Mary Bell Berry, the maker of the "Scrap Diamond" quilt. Everyone in the family worked on quilts. Mary Bell Berry, born in 1897 in Plano, Kentucky, was taught to quilt by her mother, Caroline Coleman. All of the daughters of Caroline Coleman were taught to quilt. Mary Bell Berry had three children, Otho D. Hamer, Lenora E. Hamer and Ernestine Hamer. In 1923 the family moved to Indianapolis, and later Mary Bell married Robert Berry. Ernestine Hamer Bates wrote:

I can remember in the wintertime, we all would be working on quilts. I, Ernestine, was the youngest and my mother would have me making running stitches near the edges because my arms were too short. Mother had the quilt rolled on two wood poles and tied to one pair of horses. She would have the quilt as the top, and a filling next, then the lining. Then you would have to make running stitches, slanting. We had a way of working together as follows:
> *Robert Berry-Stepfather-longest arms.*
> *Mary Berry-Mother-next longest arms.*
> *Otho Hamer-Brother-next longest arms.*
> *Lenora Hamer-sister-next longest arms.*
> *Ernestine Hamer-shortest arms.*

The "Scrap Diamond" quilt made by Mary Bell Berry, circa 1940, contains an amazing array of different cotton print fabrics. When she placed the prints in juxtaposition, with no intervening sashing, a definite block pattern was not readily discernible. Close examination, however, reveals Mary Bell Berry's quite formal organization in what appears to be a wildly informal quilt. She used a diamond one-patch and within the diamond patch one side mirrors the other. "Scrap Diamond" quilt was quilted by its present owner, Mary Lou Mollette. (Figure #23)

Mary Bell Berry. (1897-1976), Indianapolis, Indiana, was an experienced quiltmaker. Everyone in the Berry family, mother, stepfather, a son and two daughters, worked at the quilting frames. Each person's position at the frames was determined by the length of his arms. Portrait of Mary Bell Berry drawn by George Mollette.

Diagram of a diamond showing Mary Bell Berry's organization of small panels of different print fabrics within a single patch. When she constructed additional diamond patches using a multitude of different prints, the diamond shape was obscured. Drawing by George R. Mollette.

Occasionally we see a quilt that so truly epitomizes its time we are awestruck. The memories of the tumultuous 1960s and early 1970s, of "Freedom Marches," "Freedom Rides," lunch counter sit-ins, terrifying voter registration drives, murders, bombings, killing of little children, vicious attacks on protestors by police force dogs, cross burnings by the Ku Klux Klan, the courage of Rosa Parks, the charismatic, articulate, non-violence adherent Martin Luther King, Jr., the thousands of people determined to obtain their long denied civil rights, all come flooding back when I look at the "Freedom Quilt," of Jessie Telfair, Parrot, Georgia. When the first Telfair "Freedom Quilt," made in 1975, appeared in the Bicentennial exhibition of the Georgia Council for the Arts and Humanities, it had an immediate emotional impact. What a powerful quilt! No book, no speech, no banner, no sermon expressed more movingly or graphically the aspirations of African-Americans than did Jessie Telfair's "Freedom" quilt. Was it irony or patriotism that induced her to make the quilt in America's colors, red, white and blue? The exhibition quilt is the third "Freedom" quilt made by Jessie Telfair, all alike, and is dated 1980. (Figure #24)

During the 1960s, as an off-shoot of President Lyndon Johnson's humanistic "Great Society" programs, a number of poor white, black and native American rural women were organized into self-help quilt cooperatives or quilt cottage industries. One of the first, organized in 1966, was the Freedom Quilting Bee, Gees Bend, Alabama, an African-American quilting cooperative. These women, under the leadership of Estelle Witherspoon, received national acclaim for their quilts, sold in major stores in places far away from Alabama. Sales of their quilts resulted in vastly improved living conditions for the quiltmakers in their Alabama homes. Twenty-five years later, the group, currently titled the Martin Luther King, Jr., Freedom Quilting Bee, is still a viable quiltmaking cooperative, although reduced in income. Stores that formerly sold Freedom Quilting Bee quilts have opted for cheaper quilts made in the "American style" from Haiti and the Philippines.[7] A number of the other early quilt cooperatives disbanded when government financing was no longer available and difficulties were encountered when minimum wage laws were enforced. Quiltmaking is labor-intensive; and if workers must be paid by the hour, the prices of the quilts would become so expensive that sales would be drastically reduced. The International Ladies Garment Workers Union's strong opposition to working in the home did not take into consideration the special circumstances of the quilt cooperatives and so presented another problem for the groups.[8]

However, the quilt cooperative movement did not end completely with the loss of the federal government's sponsorship, as in a few instances state governments have lent limited assistance to the efforts. New African-American quilt cottage industries such as *Arkansas Country Quilts* from east central Arkansas and a recently established group in Tutweiler, Mississippi, organized somewhat differently from the earlier quilt cooperatives are making quilts for sale.

"The Coat of Many Colors" quilt, circa 1980, by the Martin Luther King, Jr., Freedom Quilting Bee is one of the few quilt patterns continually maintained in the Bee's inventory since 1972. (Figure #25)

Respect and admiration for ancient African civilizations and for the arts, crafts and traditions of Africans are no longer the sole province of professional archeologists, anthropologists, and historians. Many ordinary American black citizens, expressing a desire to explore their African backgrounds, have journeyed to Nigeria, Ghana, Sierre Leone, Kenya, Egypt, Namibia, Mozambique, and other African countries. African-Americans, aware of the distorted picture of Africa seen in much of America's films, electronic and print media, have a focused interest in things African. Quilters are making conscious and deliberate efforts to incorporate African themes in their works. Some persons begin by using African textiles in their quilts; others take courses in art history or engage in ambitious projects such as researching design traditions in a specific African tribe. Characteristic of numerous late twentieth century African-Americans, whether they make quilts or not, is the eager quest for information about the whole of the African continent.

Carole Harris of Detroit, an art major from Wayne State University, has been making quilts since the late 1960s and has acquired a national reputation for her quiltworks, which are always original and innovative. For some time her spare, minimalist, creatively pieced quilts recorded her responses to the black experience in America. Long before President George Bush announced his "New World Order," Carole Harris constructed her beautiful and optimistic (for blacks) quilt, "New World A-Coming." She has been studying intensively the design traditions of Africa and remarked, "This seems to be the answer to questions I didn't know I had." As she delved into the topic she felt an instant bonding, an uncanny sense of recognition. So stimulated was Carole Harris that she planned to make a series of quilts she would call the "Memory" series, based on an African aesthetic. The first quilt made in the series is the exhibition quilt "Reclamation," begun on February 11, 1990, the day Nelson Mandela was released from prison. Carole Harris recalls that was "a very moving experience" for her. After Harris made "Reclamation," she saw pictures of the Gelede dance costumes of the Western Yoruba and was again astonished. The Gelede dance ceremonial mask headdress is composed of a multitude of colorful, loose hanging cloth strips. When the complex rhythmic patterns of the dancing become more frenzied, the strips become airborne and swirl about the dancer's head, presenting a labyrinth of stunningly beautiful colors. How similar to "Reclamation's" construction, the same mass of vari-colored cloth strips. Her feeling of deep kinship with the African tradition increased, and she knew her "Memory" series of quilts would take her in the right direction. The body of the "Reclamation" quilt is a black fabric which dramatizes the vibrant colors of the free-hanging cloth strips. (Figure #26)

Anonymous African-American family photographed in their yard with a pieced strip quilt used as a backdrop; early twentieth century. A number of photographs, frequently from the American South, showing both black and white families with quilts used as backdrops, have been found. Photograph in the collection of Barbara Brackman.

Dorothy Nelle Sanders, Wauwatosa, Wisconsin, born in Atlanta, did not come from a quiltmaking family. She sews and has sewn quilts, both pieced and appliqued. Since the early 1970s, however, Dorothy Nelle Sanders has concentrated on designing quilts and expanding her creativity by varying her quiltmaking techniques. At present her preferred modalities are hand painting on fabric and silk screening. Introduced to African designs in art classes, she embarked on a study of African artifacts, eventually focusing on African masks. Her hand painted quilt, "African Mask Adaptation," demonstrates how attuned she was to the dissimilar designs of the many masks; how she transferred the various elements to her quilt, maintaining the essence of the originals while developing an entirely different concept. Prior to making the quilt, Dorothy Nelle Sanders had hand painted a large piece of fabric that she decided would be the lining for her "African Mask Adaptation" quilt. Her long time friend Luella Jones hand quilted it. (Figure #27)

As an aid to improving the reading skills of African-American pupils at P. S. 48, Jamaica, New York, the school's librarian and a quilter, Jean Linden, instituted a program of quiltmaking entitled "Read It and Quilt It." Fifth grade students would be taught to make pictorial quilts based on stories they had read. The children responded enthusiastically to the project, and they began to make a series of story quilts. Both objectives of the program were met successfully; the children's reading skills improved, and the pictorial quilts they made were exceptional. So impressed were the parents by the students' quilts that a request was made to Jean Linden to teach the adults quiltmaking. The parents also wanted to make pictorial quilts. After discussion, they decided to make a quilt of "The Clever Turtle," one of the *Uncle Remus Tales* by Joel Chandler Harris. Harris was not the author of the stories; he simply recorded tales told to him by black people on southern plantations. In reality, the stories were African folk tales, and the counterparts of many of the "Uncle Remus" stories have been found in African lore. When the parents of the children of P. S. 48 made "The Clever Turtle" quilt, they very pointedly made the figures African people. (Figure #28)

Lillian Beattie's quilts are instantly charming. Who else would have the talent to cut pictures from such mundane and hackneyed sources as comic strips, advertisements and magazines, make patterns from them, use the patterns to cut cloth, sprinkle the cloth people and animals across a quilt top, and so produce an exemplary work of folk art? The late Lillian Beattie, Chattanooga, Tennessee, was born November 11, 1879, in Athens, Tennessee. Not until Mrs. Beattie visited the 1939 New York World's Fair did she begin the program of quiltmaking which was later to bring fame to her and joy to others . At the World's Fair she saw geometric pieced quilts. Mrs. Beattie believed those quilts had a definite deficiency: there were no people on them. Her quilts remedied that deficiency. They are replete with people and animals, often shown in action poses, and so her quilts appear to teem with life. Evidently, Mrs. Beattie regarded her quilts as a special kind of work, reserved for expressing her creativity and humor. When visiting her once, I saw her own bed. It was neatly covered with a very simple bedcover, seamed in long panels, each panel a different muted color. I asked her if she had made the cover, and she replied yes.

On her "People of the World" quilt, some intriguing images are: a dark Scottie dog with bright red ears, tail and tongue frightening a black cat whose tail is aloft; an obese little boy clinging precariously to a slender tree limb; a stylish red check elephant with a low slung black belt and red and black cap; and the rich girl Mrs. Beattie said, "Who has so much money, she's just throwing it around." Mrs. Beattie died in 1988 at the age of 109. (Figure #29)

A person who at age nine vowed she would never make another quilt is today a creative quiltmaker, designer and teacher. Dorothy Holden, Charlottesville, Virginia, born in Kansas City, Missouri, was taught quiltmaking by her mother, a home economics teacher. That first pink and green "Nine Patch" quilt was the bane of her existence, as her daily "quilting stint" kept her from going outside to play with the other children. When Dorothy Holden resumed her quiltmaking about fifteen years ago, she favored traditional quilts, but even then she always inserted an odd quirk, "a little Dorothy in them," she reports. At present, Dorothy Holden's quilts are drawn from her fertile imagination; but she does insist the underpinnings of all her work are traditional concepts. One specialty of hers is the making of portrait quilts although she never confines herself to a single mode.

For five or six years Dorothy Holden taught integrated classes of children to make quilts in her home, and the children produced some remarkable pieces. A friend gave her a large number of bow ties. Like most quilters she collects fabrics of all kinds, but she was puzzled as to what could be done with men's old bow ties. Not stymied for very long, in 1990 she made "Have A Seat," a quilt that expressed both her ingenuity and her own hospitable manner. Although bow ties are used extensively on "Have A Seat," one has to look closely to discover them. (Figure #30)

Dr. Carolyn Mazloomi, Cincinnati, Ohio, born in Louisiana, had no quiltmaking in her family background. A self-taught quiltmaker, she began by making very traditional kinds of quilts, using that practice to perfect the technical skills essential to fine quiltmaking. During the process she learned she had an especial affinity for the quilting stitch. Using the lap quilting method because she believed she exerted more control when not depending on the tension of the quilting frames, she has made whole cloth quilts of rare beauty. Having become technically proficient, Carolyn Mazloomi began to explore other avenues, devising quilts that would depict her innermost thoughts, her experiences, her creativity.

She has been inspired by the brilliant African-American artist Dr. Bill Williams from Charlottes County, Virginia. When she saw his black and white lino-cut "The Neighborhood," she thought, "That's what I want, those negative space images." Carolyn Mazloomi began a series of six hand-painted quilts, "Solid Like a Rock," the first of which was "The Family." In "The Family" quilt she is honoring the extended family that was an integral part of black family structure for such a long time. The hands represent all the caring relatives that helped to keep the family unit together. The cross and the bell represent the black church that was an important element in most black people's upbringing; the black family did draw upon the strength of the church. Love in the family is denoted by the radiating rings, and the African-American legacy of patchwork is symbolized in the patchwork borders. Carolyn Mazloomi's dramatic "The Family" quilt exudes the power, strength, interconnectedness, and love in the extended black family that was, but may now be at the brink of dissolution. "The Family" quilt is a graphic plea to African-Americans to value their rich traditions and not to let them slip away. (Figure #31)

There were no quilters in the family of Michael Cummings, either, and he traveled a long road before coming to quiltmaking. Michael Cummings, born in Los Angeles, now living in New York, was trained as an artist, attending the State University of New York. He painted huge wall surfaces, taught and organized art programs for the New York City public school system, and finally concentrated on collages. His first experience working with fabric came when he was making a banner for a banner project which was exhibited at the American Craft Museum, New York. He was coming to a crisis point in the storing of his art materials when he realized he could transfer the collage technique to cloth and make applique images. Also, the fabric could be folded and stored quite easily. In the mid-1970s Michael Cummings began to put pictorial depictions on quilts. About his "African Jazz Series, #10" (Figure #32), made in 1990, he wrote:

> African Jazz Series, twelve quilts in the series, was developed after discovering a black and white poster that showed three African jazz musicians performing in a smoke-filled room. The poster was an enlargement of a photograph. There was a hypnotic trance on each of the performers' faces. Their expressions instantly pulled me into their world of jazz. The image of Africans performing American jazz was juxtaposed, in my thoughts, with drums and slaves brought to the Americas. Yet the poster's reality was an updated statement on how Africa had adopted our art form . . . my culture. The contradictions in this poster provoked in me excitement and ritual images. My visions translated the poster's images into colorful quilts, with tactile surfaces, narrative themes, and poetical statements. Artistic references, such as Romare Bearden, Aaron Douglas, the French painter, Rousseau, and the Egungun costumes found in the Yoruba society in western Nigeria and eastern Dahomey, influenced my work.

Growing up in Chicago, Jim Smoote, a fiber artist, saw no

quilting in his immediate family. However, traveling to Grenada, Mississippi, to visit his grandparents and relatives during summer vacations, he observed a great deal of quilting. After conducting an examination of different African textiles, Jim Smoote began to print and hand paint fabrics based on his studies. Initially he quilted his printed and hand painted fabrics, then he began to probe piecing and appliquing techniques. Twenty years later, Jim Smoote's large body of work reveals the versatility of the artist. He employs with equal aplomb the methods of piecing, applique, reverse applique, quilting, hand painting and silk screening.

His quilt "La Baker" was made after Smoote read biographies, news stories and periodical articles, and saw original poster images, a documentary film, and other films about Josephine Baker, the African-American entertainer who moved to France and became an international star. His imagination was stimulated by the drawings and poster images of Josephine Baker by Paul Colin, the French artist. Josephine Baker and Paul Colin were friends, and Jim Smoote believes the sensitivity and realism of Colin's pictures of Baker can be, in part, attributed to that friendship. When Smoote began to make the "La Baker" quilt, he worked with a computer-adept friend to do the image in three sizes on her computer. After transferring the images to cloth, Jim Smoote painted them with acrylic and fabric paints. On the "La Baker" quilt, Josephine Baker is portrayed performing her "banana dance" that shocked, titillated and delighted French audiences and subsequently made her the world's most famous and highly paid entertainer of her time. (Figure #33)

Marie Wilson, Brooklyn, New York, born in Gary, Indiana, had a mother who made quilts such as the "Double Wedding Ring" and "Sunbonnet Sue." Wilson, a skillful needlewoman, produced an original line of tote bags and story-telling, wall-hanging tapestries for New York boutiques. Three of her story-telling tapestry designs were printed on textiles, fabric yardages, by a New York store, Lowenstein and Sons. It was from her originally designed, commercially produced fabric yardages that she made her first quilt in 1976.

Marie Wilson designed the setting and coordinated the assemblage of the "Weavers of Dreams" quilt. Children in schools named for Martin Luther King, Jr., nationwide, submitted blocks for the quilt. The "Weaver of Dreams" quilt was dedicated in Atlanta and installed in the Rosa Parks Room of the King Center in 1987.

Having been a New York resident for many years, Marie Wilson's fascination with that great metropolis, its history, famous structures, infinite population mixture, its foibles, follies and fancies, everything that makes New York unlike any city in the world, has resulted in several quilts chronicling her city. The "High Jinks" quilt (Figure #34), made for the Great American Quilt Festival 3 "Citiquilts" exhibition, is her latest and records:

"HIGH JINKS"
MARIE WILSON 1991
Dimensions: 60" x 74"

1. *"TOPPING OUT" — The "topping out" ceremony marks the installation of the highest beam in a skyscraper's framework. New York ironworkers usually place an American flag and an evergreen tree on that beam. According to construction industry legend, the evergreen tree will bring new life into the building. This ritual is founded on ancient social customs. In the Orient and Europe, symbolic objects placed on the roof of a new building ranged from ears of corn and saplings to ladies handkerchiefs. These objects were offered to feed the gods, or exorcise evil spirits.*

2. *PUCK BUILDING — 295 Lafayette St., New York City — has two of these statues. The building was formerly a printing plant which housed the publication, "PUCK," a satirical magazine. "And those things that best please me. That befall preposterously." (Puck — "A Midsummer Night's Dream") Sculptor: Caspar Buberl.*

3. *Even in New York, in spring, a young man's fancy turns to love.*

4. *"Alice In Wonderland" — located in Central Park, is a gift to the City of New York from the George and Margarita Delacorte Foundation. Sculptor: Jose de Creeft.*

5. *September, 1987 — "COLLEGE TOWN MONTH AT THE LIBRARIES," sponsored by The Association For a Better New York. Slogan: "New York City is a Great College Town." Sculptor: Edward Clark Potter.*

6. *August, 1974 — Phillipe Petit, a 25-year old street artist from Nemours, France, walked a tightrope between the twin towers of the World Trade Center. At that time he had also walked the towers of the Sydney Harbor Bridge in Australia and the spires of Notre Dame in Paris.*

7. *Gracie Mansion — Built about 1799 on the site of a revolutionary fort as the country house of Archibald Gracie, Scottish merchant. From 1923 to 1932 it housed The Museum of the City of New York. Since 1942 it has been the official residence of the Mayor of New York.*

8. *April, 1983 — An 84-foot inflatable King Kong was installed atop the Empire State Building to mark the 50th anniversary of the release of the movie, "King Kong."*

9. *July, 1990 — "QM," the world's largest paper boat, was berthed in the Hudson River's North Cove as a guest of the World Financial Center's "Classic and Cool on the Hudson" summertime program. Scottish sculptor George Wylie was the boat's captain and creator. The boat was made from a 120 foot by 84 foot sheet of material. A space the size of a football field was needed to fold it up and the shipbuilders had to choose a day when there was no wind. According to George, "QM" may stand for Queen Mother, Queen Mary or Question Mark. George won't tell. The floating sculpture was created as a lament for Great Britain's decline as a maritime nation.*

10. *July, 1990 — Scottish adventurer Tom McClean left New York on July 10 in the TYPHOO ATLANTIC CHALLENGER. The Typhoo is a red motor and sail boat shaped like a bottle which does about three knots per hour. Crossing the Atlantic from New York to England took 37 days. It was Tom's sixth solo trip across the Atlantic. Previous trips include a crossing in a rowboat and in the world's smallest yacht. Thyphoo's cruise was made to raise funds for the National Children's Home, an orphanage in Great Britain. He raised $950,000. After its investigation of his logs, the Guinness Book of Records will publish that Tom is the first*

man to cross the ocean in a bottle.

11. *The Red Shoes — From March through May of 1986, a 30-foot inflatable sculpture of a pair of red ballet slippers hung from the roof of the Brooklyn Academy of Music. The sculpture was created by Ann Slavit.*

12. *October 1986 — During the sixth game of the 1986 World Series, Michael Sergio, a Manhattan musician, parachuted into Shea Stadium waving a banner inscribed, "Let's Go Mets."*

13. *Thanksgiving Day — Since 1927, R. H. Macy's has sponsored a Thanksgiving Day Parade.*

Marie Wilson

Historical quilt research guided the making of the sampler quilt "Afro-American Women and Quilts," 1979, by the author. (Figure #35) Each sampler block on "Afro-American Women and Quilts" recorded a different quilt originally made by an African-American. The goal was to substantiate the lengthy participation of African-Americans in quiltmaking by replicating blocks from black-made quilts from the ante-bellum period to the present. In the corner of each sampler quilt block embroidered in white thread is the date when the original quilt was made. Seven blocks are facsimiles of nineteenth century black-made quilts, five blocks were reproduced from twentieth century sources. Ten blocks represented quilts from southern states, two from northern states. All replicated blocks faithfully reproduced the piecing or appliqueing techniques of the original quilts except one. Block #10, "Lady's Shoe" sampler block, is appliqued; the original quilt from which the sampler block was duplicated was pieced.

Below is a listing of the original quilts and their dates, from which the sampler quilt blocks were derived:

AFRO-AMERICAN WOMEN AND QUILTS
(An Historical Sampler Quilt)

Beginning at top, left to right.
1. *Unnamed pieced block. Arkansas, ca. 1920. Original quilt*

70

made by mother of Tommie Brooks. Owner — Mrs.
Tommie Brooks, St. Louis, Missouri.

2. *Bible quilt block — "John the Baptist Baptizing Jesus Christ."*
   Georgia, ca. 1890. Original quilt made by Harriet Powers,
   Athens, Georgia. Quilt presently housed in National Mu-
   seum of American History, Smithsonian Institution, Wash-
   ington, D. C.

3. *Unnamed applique block. Plantation near Gastonia, South*
   Carolina, ca. 1850. Original quilt made by slave labor for the
   great-grandmother of Mrs. Mary Abernathy. Owner —
   Mrs. C. Bell, Columbus, Ohio.

4. *May Apple quilt block, Gees Bend, Alabama. 1967.*
   Original quilt made by the Freedom Quilting Bee, Alabama.
   This group was one of America's first quilting cooperatives,
   organized in 1966 as part of the "Great Society" economic
   and humanistic efforts.

5. *Star cradle quilt block. Boston, Massachusetts, 1836.*
   Original quilt was sold at the Boston Female Anti-Slavery
   Society's fund-raising Ladies' Fair, December 1836. Poem
   inscribed on the original quilt, in indelible ink, expressed
   Abolitionists' sentiments.

   > *Mother! when around your child*
   > *You clasp your arms in love,*
   > *And when with grateful joy you raise*
   > *Your eyes to God above —*
   > *Think of the negro-mother,*
   > *When her child is torn away —*
   > *Sold for a little slave — oh, then*
   > *For that poor mother, pray!*

6. *W. P. A. Tulip block. Kentucky, ca. 1935. Original quilt*
   made by Minnie Benberry, Grand Rivers, Kentucky. One of
   a group of like-designed quilts, made from a pattern brought to
   western Kentucky by a W. P. A. worker during the Great
   Depression. Owner — Cuesta Benberry, St. Louis, Mis-
   souri.

7. *Buzzard's Roost block. Pattern from a slave cabin quilt. The adaptation has quilted in the center patch an authentic African bird design, representing a buzzard.*

8. *Parasol Vine block. Kentucky, 1872. Original design of an anonymous black woman. Her quilt had printed fabric for stems and leaves.*

9. *Rob Peter to Pay Paul, or Dolly Madison Workbox block. Virginia, 1848. Original quilt made by Sarah Harris, who was permitted to put a date and her name on the quilt. This was so unusual it was reported in Historic Quilts by Florence Peto, p. 204. Mrs. Peto also used this pattern for the dust jacket and end papers of Historic Quilts.*

10. *Lady's Shoe block. Kentucky, 1890. Original quilt made by Fanny Cork, Grand Rivers, Kentucky. Owner — Cuesta Benberry, St. Louis, Missouri.*

11. *Strippy quilt block. Missouri, 1980. Made to represent the African design heritage apparent in some African-American women's quilts. In West Africa, weavers working on narrow looms produced narrow cloth strips, which were then pieced together for width. This construction, and especially its improvisational form, has influenced some African-American women to make a distinctive type of pieced quilt.*

12. *Mammy quilt block. Illinois, ca. 1940-1950. Original quilt made by Annette Barrigher for her first grandchild. Contrast the character of this design with the commercial stereotypical Mammy patterns, often caricatures, seen on pot holders, tea towels, toaster covers, dolls, etc. Owner — Nancy Sublett, Wheaton, Illinois.*

Cuesta Benberry

1. "History Quilt Club Prepares Unique Display," *Negro History Bulletin*, (April 1953); "Monuments and Landscapes," *Ebony Magazine*, (September 1963), p. 110; Van Shears, "The Quilting Craze Goes On . . . And On," *Home Magazine, The Los Angeles Times*, (20 January 1974), pp. 11-12.

2. "In Thanks," *Jet Magazine*, (23 May 1968); *Patch In Time*, (Mill Valley, California: Mill Valley Quilt Authority, 1972), p. 1, exhibition catalogue; " A Patch in Time," *Quilter's Newsletter Magazine*, (November 1972), p. 13.

3. Pat Flynn Kyser, "Pieces and Patches," *Quilt World*, (February 1983; August 1985).

4. Interview of Marian Thomas Berry, manager of the Douglass School Apartments, Webster Groves, Missouri, by the author, May 1982.

5. Extensive correspondence from Mrs. Jenna Benton (local historian of Garland, Texas, a relative by marriage to Mrs. Lizzie Shavers, one of the Garland High School Commemorative Quilt's makers) to the author supplied the necessary documentation for the quilt, July 1991. We thank Mrs. Benton for her vital information.

6. Ernestine Hamer Bates, personal letter, June 1991.

7. Emergency Fund Donation announcement and accompanying copied article "From Civil Rights Came Quilting Business" by Jane Davenport, n. s., n. d., circulated by Freedom Quilting Bee, circa 1989; Nancy Callahan, "Hard Times for Freedom Quilters," *The Christian Century*, (22-29, March 1989), pp. 317-318; "Ladies of the Quilt," *Craft News*, (March 1988), n. p.; Adam Nossiter, "Patches of Pride," *Atlanta Journal — Atlanta Constitution*, (6 February 1989).

8. Peter Breslow, "The End of Rural Arts and Crafts," *Country Journal*, (June 1986) pp. 16-18.
   (Taped interviews of all twentieth century quiltmakers and/or lenders of exhibition quilts were conducted by the author, April 1991 to July 1991.)

Chapter 9: Artists and Authors

In my efforts to confirm historically the pervasive presence of quilts in the lives of African-Americans, I investigated the quilt-related works of painters, sculptors, poets, novelists, and essayists. If quiltmaking had permeated the black family structure to the extent we believed it had, would it not manifest itself in black arts and literature? The inclusion of materials from these African-American visionary creators did satisfy my documentation needs, but the original intent of my research was considerably altered by some of the material encountered. Embracing the African-American quilt-oriented art and literature changed the contours of my study giving it a broader dimension, a memorable aesthetic imagery, and an enriching perspective.

Romare Bearden, New York, an important twentieth-century artist, painter, collagist and songwriter, was born in Charlotte, North Carolina. His family moved to New York City — to Harlem — when he was quite young. He spent part of his youth in Pittsburgh but would return to Mecklenburg County, North Carolina, during the summers to visit his grandparents. Those formative years in Mecklenburg County left Bearden with an indelible memory of quilts and quiltmaking. Bearden wrote:

> This mosaic Quilting Time *represents memories of many occasions in Charlotte and Mecklenburg County, North Carolina, where I lived as a child.*
>
> *. . . Women would bring various pieces of cloth they'd saved . . . When a specific pattern such as a diamond shape, was decided upon, they would rule it out on the cloth with chalk or a heavy pencil. After this they cut the material to fit those rather abstract shapes. I've seen such decorations on the centers of quilts. Also, flower and tree designs were often chosen; a head of Abraham Lincoln was extremely popular.*
>
> *It may have come to me in selecting a quilting bee (as these affairs were often called) as my subject that the technique had something to do with my own use of the medium of collage. After all, working in collage was precisely what the ladies were doing . . .*[1]

Bearden did express his thoughts and memories of quilts in the medium of collage, such as the arresting *Patchwork Quilt* of 1970 which portrays a serene nude black figure lying on a colorful scrap quilt or the *Patchwork Quilt* of 1969 which depicts a woman readying herself for a bath. Dr. Mary Schmidt Campbell suggests this is one of Bearden's series

74

of "purification" collages.[2] His masterful *Maquette for Quilting Time* (1985) pictures an old fashioned quilting party, complete with a musician, although Bearden stated, "I must confess, however, I never saw anyone playing music at a quilting bee."[3] Bearden's lithograph *Quilting Time* (1981) is a more intimate depiction of a couple, the woman sewing on a quilt and a man seated nearby assisting her.[4] Bearden, who died in 1988, left a monumental body of work of which his quilt-themed collages are a small but significant part. Bearden's own words tell us that.

Dr. John Biggers, Houston, Texas, distinguished African-American artist, author and teacher, was born in Gastonia, North Carolina. In 1957 he began to travel to West Africa to study African art and culture. What he learned there and how it synchronized with African-American culture determined the direction his art would take. In his search for the archetypes of his culture, certain images (the family, the black woman, the elders, the children) and certain objects (the anvil, the iron pot, the shotgun house, the quilt) are explored and depicted repeatedly. A reviewer wrote:

> *The rigor and stability, for instance, so evident in the patterns of a patchwork quilt becomes overlaid in a Biggers drawing with an expansive geometry, humane in its basis and eternal in its significance . . . His explorations of the possibilities of shaped canvases based upon patterns from his mother's quilt illustrates well how the artist coupled the abstract concept of form with the very real act of "piecing together" small elements to form a larger composition. In several of his works, the shotguns become "patches" which come together to form a "quilt community."* [5]

An examination of the works of John Biggers reveals how completely he has internalized concepts we would attribute to quilt construction, but in this artist's hands those concepts have become completely integrated into the whole; indeed, "a quilt community." Noteworthy examples are Biggers' *Four Sisters* (1986) and *Patchwork Quilts and Shotguns.*[6]

Paul Goodnight, Boston, prominent painter and ceramist, was born in Chicago. He received his art education at the Massachusetts College of Art, graduating in 1975. Goodnight, a Vietnam veteran, has traveled widely to such places as Haiti, Brazil, Nicaragua, Soviet Armenia, East and West Africa. All of the experiences from those journeys have flowed into his art. We can see some of his responses to West African

culture in his painting *Links and Lineage* (1986). (Figure A, p. 81) Three
generations of an African-American family are depicted, the eldest
member sewing on a most unusual quilt. The quilt blocks shown are not
traditional American patchwork quilt block designs; rather, each block is
a traditional African tribal design from the Yoruba, the Dogon, the Ewe,
the Ashanti, and other African tribes. *Links and Lineage* was commissioned by the Massachusetts Middlesex Chapter of the Links Inc., a
national organization of African-American women that promotes the
awareness, exploration, and history of African-American culture. They
requested that Goodnight reflect in the painting the image and the values
of the Links organization. *Links and Lineage* was so admired that the
Hallmark Company of Kansas City, Missouri, purchased the rights to
reproduce it as a Christmas card. Paul Goodnight's painting *The
Quiltmakers* (1987) reiterates the multi-generational African-American
family's bond with quiltmaking.

An ambitious project entitled *Murals, Masters and Monuments*
is underway to build dual monuments celebrating Africans and African-
Americans, one to be installed in Mozambique, East Africa, and one in
the United States. On the interior walls of the monument will be four
painted quilts, one for each season of the year. Paul Goodnight is the
producer of the American monument project.[7]

In contrast to the trained African-American artists such as
Bearden, Biggers, and Goodnight, Horace Pippin was a folk artist who left
school at age 14 and later enlisted in the Army.

> *During World War I a sniper wounded him in the right shoulder,*
> *partially paralyzing his arm. After the war . . . he also began to*
> *paint — laboriously. He would clasp the brush in his deadened right*
> *hand, then use his left arm to push hand and brush across the*
> *surface of the canvas.*[8]

Horace Pippin's *The Domino Players* (1943) shows in the background a
black-clad elderly woman sewing a log cabin quilt in the "Courthouse
Steps" pattern. Vari-colored fabric scraps, scissors and thread lie on the
floor beside her chair.[9] *The Domino Players* is a study in black, grey and
white with touches of red. "Pippin was a connoisseur of monochrome . . .
As an intimate diarist of black life, Pippin painted what he knew . . ."[10]

The Satimbe Society (1990) is a commemorative painting by
Tyrone Geter. (Figure B, p. 81) He wrote:

The mask and its many functions among numerous African tribes has been traditionally the private domain of the male members of the tribe. There are only a few examples where women have been mask-wearing participants in tribal ceremonies.

The Satimbe mask (tall center one) from which this painting takes its name represents the first woman allowed to join the Dogon Society of Masks. It denotes the respected and dignified role of women in Dogon culture. Other symbols and their meanings are: the snake representing speed of movement, and sometimes death; the lizard means long life and reproduction; the tortoise denotes old age, wisdom, and perseverance; the Ashanti golden stool is believed by the Ashanti people to be a gift from God, and therefore sacred; the Aka mask is a funeral and ceremonial mask from the Cameroons.

The painting The Satimbe Society *salutes the dignity, strength, and respect due the African-American woman. The African-American woman, like women in every culture, has historically been the glue that has held the Black family together. Her central role in the survival and growth of the Black family is a monument to the perseverance and struggle of a people against almost insurmountable odds. It is the stuff from which legends spring.*

Tyrone Geter, Akron, Ohio, a renowned artist, born in Alabama, received both his B. F. A and M. F. A degrees from the University of Ohio. His paternal and maternal grandmothers were quiltmakers, and today his mother continues to make quilts. He remembers the many casually constructed, utilitarian scrap quilts made by his family. Geter lived in Nigeria for nearly seven years, and while there absorbed much of the culture of that West African country. He noticed that various African fabrics were reminiscent of the patchwork quilts he had seen in America where early on he had developed an appreciation for textiles, patterns and handwork. Although Tyrone Geter did not see any quilts in Nigeria, the presence of actual African patchwork quilts had been reported in western sources as early as the 1890s. Mary Kingsley in her 1897 book *Travels in West Africa* wrote:

> *Few prettier sights have I seen than those on that sandbank — the merry brown forms dancing or lying stretched on it: gaudy colored patchwork quilts and chintz mosquito bars that have been washed, spread and drying, looking from Kangwe on the hill above, like beds*

of bright flowers.

An 1890 issue of *Harper's Bazar* contained a feature of a missionary teaching African girls to make patchwork. For many years printed cotton fabric believed to have typical African designs was manufactured in Europe and was then exported to Africa. Geter noted that now, in addition to producing the hand woven textiles indigenous to West Africa, the printed cotton trade fabric formerly produced in Europe is being manufactured in Africa by the Africans. However, Geter especially favors the hand woven African fabrics and used kente cloth as a background in his painting *Malaiki*. He wrote:

> *The painting* Malaiki (1991) *links the African-American experience with their African origins. Malaiki utilizes African motifs to weave a spirit of unity and harmony of African and African-American culture. It simply states we cannot be one without the other.*

Varnette P. Honeywood, nationally known artist, born in Los Angeles, graduated as an art major from Spelman College and later received a Master's Degree in Education from the University of Southern California. Her frequent visits, during childhood, to the homes of relatives in Mississippi and Louisiana imbued her with a strong sense of the rich black traditions of the rural South. Varnette Honeywood has internalized the varied, rhythmic textile traditions of Africa, and her art is motivated by the colorful appliques of Dahomey, the blue resist dye fabrics, the Kente cloth. Her arresting collage *She Who Teaches, Learns* has a background similar to the "Broken Dishes" quilt pattern, but Honeywood's source was African. A recognizably traditional quilt, a scrap string star, does cover the marriage bed in her *I Do Thee Wed*. So, too, is there a traditional quilt, "Double Wedding Ring," in the Honeywood collage, *A Century of Empowerment*, commissioned by *Essence Magazine* for its fifteenth anniversary. Honeywood stated:

> *The important thing is that we draw on Africa for inspiration in symbolism and technique . . . The exciting thing is that the African-American artists are coming into their own. I think it's time we recognize our own visual history.*[11]

An African-American who successfully and uniquely synthesized quiltmaking and painting techniques is Faith Ringgold, New York, noted artist, art professor and ardent feminist. Faith Ringgold, born in New York City, received her art education at City College. For many years she garnered praise for her painted canvases, her masks and dolls. In the early 1980s Faith Ringgold combined her painting with quiltmaking and developed an original and unique concept — the painted story quilt. The text of a story is written on the quilt, illustrated by painted pictures, all enclosed within patchwork borders. Since her first painted story quilt, *Who's Afraid of Aunt Jemima?*, Ringgold's colorful, imaginative and frequently humorous narrative quilts have captured the public's attention. Especially appealing are the story quilts that relate her experiences growing up in Harlem. One of her most wondrous painted story quilts, *Tar Beach*, was recently adapted for a story book.[12] Faith Ringgold remembers the warm summer evenings when the family would go up on the rooftop — tar beach — for fun and relaxation, a magical time for her to dream, to imagine wonderful and exciting experiences.

African-American literary works have been inspired by quiltmaking. Whether the authors, being quiltmakers themselves, wrote from personal perspectives or whether they recorded quilting they had observed, quilts seem to be very special to them. Paul Laurence Dunbar, one of America's first black poets to acquire national popularity in the nineteenth century, wrote a tender love poem, *The Quilting*, in 1890. Mary Effie Newsome, a participant in the Harlem Renaissance of the 1920s-1930s, composed the poem, *The Quilt*, in 1927. *Homespun Heroines* (1926) by Ohioan Hallie Quinn Brown often mentioned quilts in the biographical essays of the black women cited, many of whom were her intimate friends. Alice Walker, the award-winning novelist, poet and essayist grew up in a quiltmaking environment and is herself a quiltmaker. It seems inevitable that the characters Celie and Sofia in the novel *The Color Purple* (1982) were described jointly making a quilt. In two essays in her book *In Search of Our Mother's Gardens* (1983), quilts figure prominently; and quilts are central to the plot of Walker's short story "Everyday Use" from the book *In Love and Trouble* (1983). Walker's emotional responses to quilts set her apart from other authors; few capture the true meaning of quilts as does she. *Jubilee* (1966), a novel by Margaret Walker, contains an account of a nineteenth century quilting bee. Valerie Flournoy's *The Patchwork Quilt* (1985), a book of juvenile fiction about a black family's experience with quilting, is further enhanced by the illustrations of the famous African-American medalist, artist Jerry Pinkney.[13]

For a very long time, quiltmaking has penetrated deeply into the fabric of African-American society. Yet our research of black-made quilts is just a little beyond the selvedges of that fabric. We must cut more deeply into that fabric. They deserve no less — those multitudes of black quiltmakers whose works have largely gone unrecorded — for they have always maintained an African-American presence in American quilts.

1. Romare Bearden, "Artist's Statement," *Maquette for Quilting Time*, (Detroit Institute of Art, 1984).
2. Kinshasha Holman Conwill, *Memory and Metaphor: The Art of Romare Bearden, 1940-1987*, (New York: Studio Museum of Harlem, Oxford University Press, 1991), p. 63.
3. Bearden, "Artist's Statement."
4. *Idem.*, "Quilting Time," (Lithograph: Vlepis Interests, Co., 1981).
5. Alvia J. Wardlow, *John Biggers: Patchwork Quilts and Shotguns*, (Houston, Texas: Transco Gallery, 1987), exhibition catalogue.
6. *Ibid.*, p. 2.
7. Taped interview with Paul Goodnight, 20 May 1991.
8. Mark Stevens, "Pippin's Folk Heroes," *Newsweek* (22 August 1977), p. 59.
9. Phillips Collection, Washington, D. C.
10. Stevens, p. 60.
11. Varnette Honeywood, *Traditions: She Who Teaches Learns; The Art of Varnette Honeywood*, (Atlanta: Spelman College, 1987), exhibition catalogue.
12. Faith Ringgold, *Tar Beach*, (New York: Crown Pub., 1991).
13. Paul Laurence Dunbar, "The Quilting," *Complete Poems of Paul Laurence Dunbar*; Mary Effie Newsome, "The Quilt," *Carolling Dusk*, (New York: Harper Brothers, 1927); Hallie Quinn Brown, *Homespun Heroines and Other Women of Distinction*, (Xenia, Ohio: Alden Pub., 1926); Margaret Walker, *Jubilee*, (Boston: Houghton, Mifflin, 1966); Valerie Flournoy, *The Patchwork Quilt*, (New York: Dial Books, E. P. Dutton, 1985).

    Alice Walker, *The Color Purple*, (New York: Harcourt Brace Jovanovich, 1982); ———, *In Search of Our Mothers' Gardens: Womanist Prose*, (San Diego: Harcourt Brace Jovanovich, 1983); ———, "Everyday Use," *In Love and Trouble: Stories of Black Women*, (New York: Harcourt Brace Jovanovich, 1973); ———, *The Alice Walker Calendar for 1986*, (San Diego: Harcourt Brace Jovanovich, 1986), shows a detail of ". . . my *Color Purple* quilt."

Figure A

Figure B

Figure A, Links and Lineage, by Paul Goodnight, Boston, Massachusetts, 37 1/2 x 27 1/2 inches. The artist adapted various African tribal design motifs for the quilt blocks. Original painting commissioned by the Massachusetts Middlesex Chapter of the Links, Inc. and is in their permanent collection. Photograph courtesy of the artist.

Figure B, The Satimbe Society, by Tyrone Geter, Akron, Ohio, 1990, 19 1/2 x 22 1/2 inches. Original painting in the collection of the artist. Photograph courtesy of the artist.

Figure 1, Reel Quilt, also called Star Quilt by owner, made by slave labor on plantation, Sedalia, Missouri, dated 1844, 113 x 104 inches, cotton, pieced. Twenty-five blocks. Collection of Mrs. William Miller.

Figure 2, Original Whig Rose Quilt, made by slave labor on the White family plantation near Richmond, Kentucky, circa 1860, 102 x 82 1/2 inches, cotton, appliqued, pieced. Twenty blocks. Collection of Suellen and Richard Meyer.

Figure 3, Tulip Quilt, made by Ann, a sixteen-year-old slave on the plantation of Captain and Mrs. William Womack, Pittsylvania County, Virginia, circa 1840, 100 x 85 inches, cotton, appliqued, pieced. Thirty blocks. Collection of the Smithsonian Institution, Negative #76-13388.

Figure 4, Broderie Perse Medallion Quilt Top, (Nell Chisolm Quilt),
made by Johanna Davis, Charleston, South Carolina, circa 1845-1853,
plain cotton, glazed chintz, muslin, appliqued. Gift of Nell Houston
Chisolm. Collection of the Avery Research Center for African American
History and Culture, College of Charleston, Charleston, South Carolina.
Photograph courtesy of the Avery Research Center.

Figure 5, Framed Medallion Quilt Top, made by Frances M. Jolly,
Massachusetts or North Carolina, date inscribed 1839, 105 x 102 inches,
silk and wool, appliqued, pieced, and embellished with braid and embroidery. Collection of the Smithsonian Institution, Negative #89-10437.

Figure 6, Pineapples Quilt, made by the women of Liberia to honor Reverend James Edward East, Executive Secretary of the Foreign Mission Board, National Baptist Convention of the United States of America, 1922, 70 x 57 1/2 inches, cotton, appliqued. Inscribed on quilt is "Gift to Reverend James E. East." Four blocks. Collection of Gladys East.

Figure 7, Liberty Medallion Quilt, made by Elizabeth Hobbs Keckley, a former slave, Washington, D. C., circa 1870, 85 1/2 x 85 1/2 inches, silk, pieced, appliqued, embroidered. Collection of Ross Trump.

Figure 8, Bible Scenes Quilt, made by a member of the Drake family, Thomaston, Georgia, circa 1900-1910, 76 1/2 x 71 inches, cotton, appliqued. Four blocks. Collection of Shelly Zegart.

Figure 9, The Lord's Prayer Quilt, made by Lorraine Mahan, Philadelphia, Pennsylvania, 1974, 87 x 85 inches, cotton, appliqued. Eighteen outer and twenty-five inner blocks. Collection of Lorraine A. Mahan.

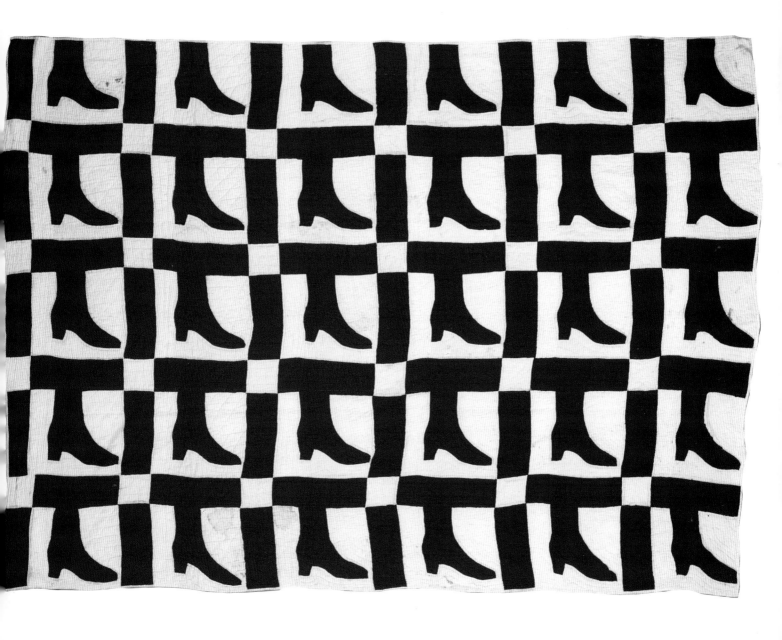

Figure 10, Lady's Shoe Quilt, made by Fanny Cork, Grand Rivers, Kentucky, circa 1890, 67 x 93 inches, cotton, pieced. Thirty blocks. Collection of Cuesta Benberry.

Figure 11, *Fleur de Lis* Quilt, made by Sara Miller, Natchez, Mississippi, circa 1900, 82 1/2 x 82 1/2 inches, cotton, appliqued. Thirty-two blocks and central medallion. Collection of Portia Robb Higgins.

Figure 12, Crazy Quilt, made by Mima Thompson Perkins, Trevilians, Virginia, circa 1888-1890, 82 x 61 inches, wool, pieced, appliqued, embroidered. Twenty blocks. Collection of the Perkins-Wilbourn family.

Figure 13, Parlor Quilt, made by Mima Thompson Perkins, Trevilians,
Virginia, circa 1890, 66 1/4 x 46 1/4 inches, wool, silk embroidery, pieced.
Thirty blocks. Collection of the Perkins-Wilbourn family.

Figure 14, Buggy Quilt, made by Mima Thompson Perkins, Trevilians, Virginia, circa 1915-1920, 74 3/4 x 74 3/4 inches, cotton, rayon, sewn unadorned crazy patch style. Collection of the Perkins-Wilbourn family.

Figure 15, Brick Pattern Quilt Top, made by Eva Perkins Ragsdale,
Trevilians, Virginia, circa 1915, 88 1/2 x 61 inches, pieced, wool flannels.
Thirty blocks. Collection of the Perkins-Wilbourn family.

Figure 16, Unnamed Pattern, Variation of the Arrowhead or Fish Block Quilt Top, made by Emma Perkins Wilbourn, Trevilians, Virginia, circa 1900-1925, 60 x 81 inches, cotton, pieced. Collection of the Perkins-Wilbourn family.

Figure 17, Album Quilt, made by Emma Perkins Wilbourn, Trevilians,
Virginia, and New York City, top, circa 1900-1925, incomplete quilting
begun many years later, 91 x 68 inches, cotton, pieced. Fifteen blocks.
Collection of the Perkins-Wilbourn family.

Figure 18, Large One Patch Squares Quilt Top, made by Eva Perkins Ragsdale, Trevilians, Virginia, circa 1940-1950, 94 1/2 x 86 1/2 inches, cotton, rayon, pieced. Fifty-six blocks. Collection of the Perkins-Wilbourn family.

Figure 19, The Four Churches Commemorative Signature Quilt Top, from the estate of Ashley Washam, makers not identified, Emporia, Kansas, inscribed both 1916 and 1930, 80 1/2 x 77 inches, cotton, embroidered. Forty blocks and center medallion square. A memorial to pastors and members of four churches, name inscriptions in turkey red embroidery. Collection of Emily Hooper.

Figure 20, Harriet Tubman Quilt, made by the Negro History Club of Marin City and Sausalito, California, 1951, 120 x 96 inches, cotton, appliqued. Designed by Ben Irvin. Gift of the Howard Thurman Educational Trust to the permanent collection of the Robert W. Woodruff Library, Atlanta University Center, Atlanta, Georgia.
Photograph couresty of the Robert W. Woodruff Library.

Figure 21, Frederick Douglass Quilt, made by the Negro History Club of Marin City and Sausalito, California, 1953, 120 x 96 inches, cotton, appliqued. Designed by Ben Irvin. Gift of the Howard Thurman Educational Trust to the permanent collection of the Robert W. Woodruff Library, Atlanta University Center, Atlanta, Georgia.
Photograph couresty of the Robert W. Woodruff Library.

Figure 22, Bowie County Bears Quilt, made by Lila Kelley-Brown and Lizzie Shavers, Garland, Texas, 1948-1949, 80 x 62 1/2 inches, cotton, appliqued. Collection of Rowland and Eleanor B. Miller.

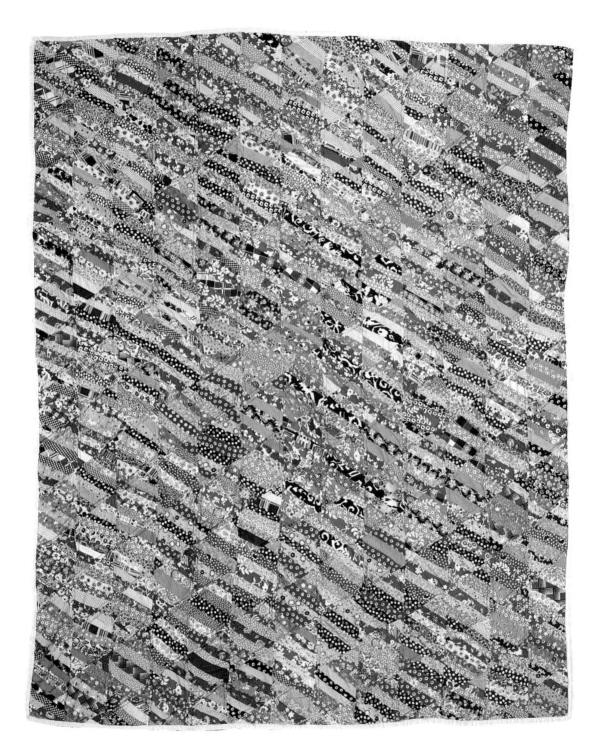

Figure 23, Scrap Diamonds Quilt, made by Mary Bell Berry, Indianapolis, Indiana, circa 1930-1940, 73 1/4 x 60 inches, cotton, pieced. Quilted by Mary Lou Mollette. Collection of Mrs. Mary Lou Harvey Mollette.

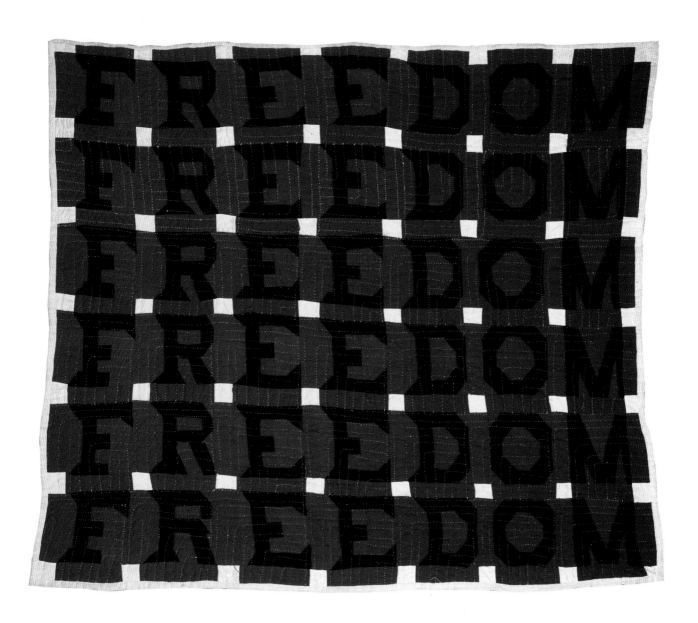

Figure 24, Freedom Quilt, made by Jessie Telfair, Parrot, Georgia, 1980, cotton, synthetic fabrics, pieced, appliqued, 73 x 85 inches. Forty-two blocks. Collection of Shelly Zegart.

Figure 25, Coat of Many Colors Quilt, made by the Martin Luther King, Jr., Quilting Bee, Gees Bend, Alabama, circa 1980, 55 x 38 inches, cotton, pieced, all-over one patch pattern. Collection of Cuesta Benberry.

Figure 26, Reclamation Quilt, Memory Series #2, made by Carole Harris, Detroit, Michigan, 1990, 72 x 50 inches, cotton, pieced. Collection of Carole Harris.

Figure 27, African Mask Adaption Quilt, made by Dorothy Nelle Sanders, Wauwatosa, Wisconsin, 1976, 68 1/2 x 86 inches, cotton, silk screened, fabric paint. Quilted by Luella Jones. Collection of the artist.

Figure 28, The Clever Turtle Quilt, made by the parents of school children at P. S. 48, Jamaica, New York, 1975, 60 x 29 1/2 inches, cotton, felt, appliqued. Seven blocks. Collection of Jean C. Linden.

Figure 29, People of the World Quilt, made by Lillian Beattie, Chattanooga, Tennessee, 1979, 71 1/2 x 54 1/2 inches, applique, and embroidery. Cotton and cotton blends. Collection of Bets Ramsey. Photograph courtesy of Williams College Museum of Art, "Stitching Memories: African Story Quilts," April 15 - October 1, 1989.

Figure 30, Have a Seat Quilt, made by Dorothy Holden, Charlottesville, Virginia, 1990, 70 x 57 inches, silk foulard, cotton, synthetic fabrics used in men's ties, pieced, appliqued. Collection of Dorothy H. Holden.

Figure 31, The Family Quilt from "Solid Like a Rock" series, made by
Carolyn Mazloomi, Cincinnati, Ohio, 1989, 49 x 39 inches, cotton, fabric
paint, pieced. Collection of the artist.

Figure 32, African Jazz Series #10 Quilt, made by Michael Cummings, New York City, 1990, 98 x 68 inches, cotton, machine appliqued. Loaned by the artist.

Figure 33, La Baker Quilt, made by Jim Smoote, Chicago, Illinois, 1990, 47 x 35 inches, cotton, acrylic paint, photo transfer pellon, appliqued. Collection of the artist.

Figure 34, High Jinks Quilt, made by Marie Wilson, Brooklyn, New York, 1990, 75 x 60 inches, cotton, pieced, appliqued. Thirteen blocks. Collection of the artist.

Figure 35, Afro-American Women and Quilts, made by Cuesta
Benberry, St. Louis, Missouri, 1979, 78 x 53 inches, cotton, pieced,
appliqued, embroidered, ink-inscribed. Twelve blocks. Collection of the
artist.

Bibliography: Part One

Andrews, William L., ed. *Sisters of the Spirit: Three Black Women's Autobiographies of the Nineteenth Century.* Bloomington: Indiana University Press, 1986.

———. *Six Women's Slave Narratives.* New York: Oxford University Press, 1988.

———. *To Tell A Free Story: The First Century of Afro-American Autobiography, 1760-1865.* Urbana: University of Illinois, 1988.

Aptheker, Herbert, ed. *A Documentary History of the Negro People in the United States: From Colonial Times Through the Civil War, Vol. 1; From Reconstruction Years to the Founding of the N.A.A.C.P. in 1910, Vol. 2.* New York: Citadel Press, 1951; Reprint Ed., 1966.

Banks, Ann, ed. *First Person America.* New York: Vintage Books, 1981.

Bardolph, Richard. *The Negro Vanguard.* New York: Holt, Rinehart and Winston, 1959.

Bennett, Lerone. *Before the Mayflower: A History of Black America.* New York: Penguin Books, 1984.

Berlin, Ira. *Slaves Without Masters: The Free Negro in the Ante-bellum South.* Oxford: Oxford University Press, 1974.

Blackburn, Robin. *The Overthrow of Colonial Slavery.* London: Verso, 1988.

Blassingame, John W. *The Slave Community.* New York: Oxford University Press, 1979.

Bontemps, Arna, ed. *Great Slave Narratives.* Boston: Beacon Press, 1969.

———. *Forever Free: Art By African-American Women, 1862-1980.* Alexandria, Virginia: Dr. Jacqueline Fonvielle Bontemps, 1980.

Boser-Sarivaxévanis, Renee. *Textilhandwerk in West Afrika.* Basel: fur Volkerkunde und Schweizerische Museum, 1973. (German Text.)

Brawley, Benjamin. *Early Negro American Writers: Selections with Biographies and Critical Introductions.* New York: Dover, 1970.

Brown, William Wells. *Clotel, or the President's Daughter,* (1853). New York: The Citadel Press, 1969.

———. *The Narrative of William W. Brown: A Fugitive Slave And A Lecture Delivered Before The Female Anti-Slavery Society of Salem, 1847.* New York: Addison-Wesley, 1969.

Butler, Broadus. *Craftsmanship: A Tradition in Black America.* New York: R. C. A., 1976.

Callahan, Nancy. *The Freedom Quilting Bee.* Tuscaloosa: University of Alabama Press, 1987.

Chase, Judith Wragg. *Afro-American Art and Craft.* New York: Van Nostrand Reinhold, 1971.

Clinton, Catherine. *The Plantation Mistress: Woman's World in the Old South.* New York: Pantheon Books, 1982.

Cowley, Malcolm, ed. *Adventures of An African Slaver Being A True Account of the Life of Captain Theodore Canot, Trader in Gold, Ivory and Slaves on the Coast of Guinea: His Own Story as Told in the Year 1854 to Brantz Mayer.* Garden City, New York: Garden City Pub., 1928.

Dendel, Esther Warner. *African Fabric Crafts: Sources of African Designs and Techniques.* New York: Taplinger, 1974.

Douglass, Frederick. *Narrative of the Life of Frederick Douglass: An American Slave.* Boston: Anti-Slavery Office, 1845. Reprint Ed.: Garden City, N. Y.: Doubleday, 1963.

DuBois, W. E. B. *Black Reconstruction in America, 1860-1880.* Reprint Ed.: New York: Atheneum, 1985.

Eicher, Joanne Bubolz. *Nigerian Handcrafted Textiles.* ILE-IFE, Nigeria: University of IFE, 1976.

Engs, Robert Francis. *Freedom's First Generation: Black Hampton, Virginia, 1861-1890.* Philadelphia: University of Pennsylvania Press, 1979.

Ferrero, Pat, Elaine Hedges, and Julie Silber. *Hearts and Hands: The Influence of Women and Quilts in American Society.* San Francisco: Quilt Digest Press, 1987.

Ferris, William, ed. *Afro-American Folk Art and Crafts.* Jackson, Mississippi: University of Mississippi, 1983.

Foner, Laura, and Eugene D. Genovese, eds. *Slavery in the New World: A Comparative Reader.* Englewood Cliffs, N. J.: Prentice-Hall, 1969.

Forner, Eric. *Nothing But Freedom: Emancipation and Its Legacy.* Baton Rouge: Louisiana State University Press, 1983.

Fox-Genovese, Elizabeth. *Within the Plantation Household: Black and White Women of the Old South.* Chapel Hill: University of North Carolina Press, 1988.

Franklin, John Hope. *From Slavery to Freedom: A History of Negro Americans.* New York: Alfred A. Knopf, 1947; Fifth Edition, 1980.

Gates, Henry Louis, ed. *Classsic Slave Narratives.* New York: New American Library, 1987.

Gatewood, Willard B. *Aristocrats of Color: The Black Elite, 1880-1920.* Bloomington: Indiana University Press, 1990.

Genovese, Eugene D. *The Political Economy of Slavery: Studies in the Economy and Society of the Slave South.* New York: Random House, 1967.

————. *Roll, Jordan, Roll: The World The Slaves Made.* New York: Pantheon, 1972.

Georgia Writers' Project, Savannah Unit: Work Projects Administration. Athens: University of Georgia Press, 1940.

Giddings, Paula. *When and Where I Enter: The Impact of Black Women on Race and Sex in America.* New York: William Morrow, 1984.

Graham, Shirley. *There Was Once A Slave: The Heroic Story of Frederick Douglass.* New York: Julian Messner, 1947.

Gutman, Herbert G. *The Black Family in Slavery and Freedom, 1750-1925.* New York: Random House, 1976.

Henry, Vicki, and Susan Bellan. *Tapisseries Du Lesotho, Tapestries from Lesotho.* Ufundi Gallery, Ottawa, Canada; Kingdom of Lesotho Handicrafts: Canadian International Development Agency, 1979. (French/English Text.)

Hermann, Janet Sharp. *The Pursuit of a Dream.* New York: Oxford University Press, 1981.

Herskovits, Melville J. *The Myth of the Negro Past.* Boston: Beacon Hill Press, 1958.

Hull, Gloria T., Patricia Bell Scott, and Barbara Smith, eds. *But Some of Us Are Brave: Black Women's Studies.* Old Westbury, N. Y.: The Feminist Press, 1982.

Jacobs, Harriet A. [Linda Brent]. *Incidents in the Life of a Slave Girl Written by Herself, (1857).* Reprint Ed.: Cambridge, Mass.: Harvard University Press, 1987.

Johnson, Michael P., and James L. Roark. *Black Masters: A Free Family of Color in the Old South.* New York: W. W. Norton, 1984.

Jordan, Winthrop. *White Over Black: American Attitudes Toward the Negro.* Chapel Hill: University of North Carolina Press, 1968.

Kaplan, Sidney, and Emma Nogrady Kaplan. *The Black Presence in the Era of the American Revolution.* Amherst: The University of Massachusetts Press, 1989.

Katz, William Lorenz, ed. *Five Slave Narratives.* New York: Arno Press and the *New York Times,* 1968.

Keckley, Elizabeth. *Behind the Scenes: Thirty Years A Slave And Four Years in the White House.* New York: New York Printing, 1868; Reprint Ed., Arno Press, 1968.

Kulikoff, Allan. *Tobacco and Slaves: The Development of Southern Cultures in the Chesapeake, 1680-1800.* Chapel Hill: University of North Carolina Press, 1986.

Lebsock, Suzanne. *The Free Women of Petersburg: Status and Culture in a Southern Town, 1784-1860.* New York: W. W. Norton, 1984.

Lerna, Gerda. *Black Women in White America: A Documentary History.* New York: Pantheon, 1972.

Litwack, Leon, and August Meier. *Black Leaders of the Nineteenth Century.* Urbana: Board of Trustees of the University of Illinois, 1988.

Meier, August, and Elliot Rudwick. *From Plantation to Ghetto.* New York: Hill and Wang, 1966.

Meltzer, Milton, ed. *In Our Own Words: A History of the American Negro, 1619-1865.* New York: Thomas Crowell, 1964.

Miller, Randall M. *Dear Master: Letters of a Slave Family.* Athens: University of Georgia Press, 1990.

Newman, Thelma R. *Contemporary African Arts and Crafts.* New York: Crown, 1974.

Northrup, Solomon. *Twelve Years A Slave.* Auburn: Derby and Miller, 1854. Reprint Ed., New York: Dover, 1970.

Olmsted, Frederick Law. *The Slave States.* New York: G. Putnam's Sons, 1959.

Pauli, Hertha. *Her Name Was Sojourner Truth.* New York: Avon Books, 1976.

Petry, Ann. *Harriet Tubman: Conductor on the Underground Railroad.* New York: Thomas Crowell, 1955.

Picton, John, and John Mack. *African Textiles*. London: British Museum, 1989.

Price, Sally and Richard. *Afro-American Arts of the Suriname Rain Forest*. Berkeley: University of California Press, 1980.

Papachristou, Judith. *Women Together: A History in Documents of the Women's Movement in the United States*. New York: Alfred A. Knopf, 1976.

Quarles, Benjamin. *Black Abolitionists*. New York: Oxford University Press, 1969.

Rawick, George P., ed. *The American Slave: A Composite Autobiography*. 19 Vols. Contributions in Afro-American and African Studies, No. 11. Westport, Connecticut, 1972.

Scobie, Edward. *Black Britannia: A History of Blacks in Britain*. Chicago: Johnson Publishers, 1972.

Sobel, Mechal. *The World They Made Together: Black and White Values in Eighteenth Century Virginia*. Princeton, N. J.: Princeton University Press, 1987.

Spring, Christopher. *African Textiles*. New York: Crescent Books, 1989.

Stampp, Kenneth. *The Peculiar Institution: Slavery in the Ante-Bellum South*. New York: Random House, 1956.

Still, William. *The Underground Railroad, (1872)*. Reprint Ed., Chicago: Johnson Publishers, 1970.

Tate, Thad W. *The Negro in Eighteenth Century Williamsburg*. Williamsburg, Va.: The Colonial Williamsburg Foundation, 1965.

Thompson, Robert Farris. *Flash of the Spirit: African and Afro-American Art and Philosophy*. New York: Random House, 1983.

Wade, Richard C. *Slavery in the Cities: The South, 1820-1860*. London: Oxford University Press, 1964.

White, Deborah. *Ar'nt I A Woman? Female Slaves in the Plantation South*. New York: W. W. Norton, 1985.

Wilson, Harriet E. *Our Nig or Sketches from the Life of a Free Black*. Boston: G. C. Rand and Avery, 1859; Reprint Ed., New York: Random House, 1983.

Wilson, James L. *Clementine Hunter: American Folk Artist*. Gretna: Pelican Pub., 1988.

Yeatman, Norman R., ed. *Life Under the "Peculiar Institution": Selections from the Slave Narrative Collection*. New York, 1970.

Bibliography: Part Two
Museum and Exhibition Catalogues

Baskett, Tom, ed. *Persistence of the Spirit: The Black Experience in Arkansas.* Resource Center, Arkansas Endowment for the Humanities, 1986.

Benson, Jane, and Nancy Olson. *The Power of Cloth: Political Quilts, 1845-1986.* Cupertino, Ca.: Euphrat Gallery, 1987.

Campbell, Edward, and Kym S. Rice, eds. *Before Freedom Came: African-American Life in the Antebellum South.* Charlottesville, Va.: The University Press of Virginia and the Museum of the Confederacy, 1991.

Christopherson, Katy. *The Political and Campaign Quilt.* Frankfort, Ky.: The Kentucky Heritage Quilt Society, 1984.

Clark, Ricky. *Quilts and Carousels: Folk Art in the Firelands.* Oberlin, Ohio: Firelands Association for the Visual Arts, 1983.

Flomenhaft, Eleanor. *Faith Ringgold: A 25-Year Survey.* Hempstead, N. Y.: Fine Arts Museum of Long Island, 1990.

Freeman, Roland. *Something to Keep You Warm: The Roland Freeman Collection of Black American Quilts from the Mississippi Heartland.* Jackson, Miss.: Mississippi State Historical Museum, 1981.

Fry, Gladys-Marie. *Stitched From the Soul: Slave Quilts from the Ante-Bellum South.* New York: Dutton Studio Books with the Museum of American Folk Art, 1990.

Gates, J. M. *Afro-American Heritage Quilt and Historical Exhibit: The Afro-American Bicentennial Quilt.* Portland, Or.: Oregon Historical Society, 1976.

Gilfoy, Peggy Stolz. *Patterns of Life: West African Strip Weaving Traditions.* Washington, D. C.: National Museum of African-Art, Smithsonian Institution Press, 1988.

Grudin, Eva Ungar. *Stitching Memories: African-American Story Quilts.* Williamstown, Mass.: Williams College Museum of Art, 1990.

Hammond, Leslie King. *Ritual and Myth: A Survey of African American Art.* New York: Studio Museum of Harlem, 1982.

Holstein, Jonathan, and John Finley. *Kentucky Quilts, 1800-1900.* Louisville: The Kentucky Quilt Project, Inc., 1982.

Horton, Laurel, and Lynn R. Myers. *Social Fabric: South Carolina's Traditional Quilts.* Columbia, S. C.: McKissick Museum, University of South Carolina, n.d.

Hotton, Julia. *Design Works of Bedford-Stuyvesant.* New York: Brooklyn Museum Community Gallery, 1974.

Hufford, Mary, Marjorie Hunt, and Steven Hunt. *The Grand Generation: Memeory, Mastery, Legacy.* Seattle: Smithsonian Institution Traveling Exhibition Service with University of Washington Press, 1987.

Lamb, Venice and Alastair. *West African Narrow Strip-Weaving.* County Borough of Halifax, Canada: Halifax Museums, 1973.

Lebsock, Suzanne, and Kym S. Rice. *A Share of Honour: Virginia Women, 1600-1945.* Richmond: The Virginia Women's Cultural History Project, 1984.

Leon, Eli. *Who'd A Thought It: Improvisation in African-American Quiltmaking.* San Francisco: San Francisco Craft and Folk Art Museum, 1987.

Livingston, Jane, and John Beardsley with Regina Perry. *Black Folk Art in America, 1930-1980.* Corcoran Gallery, Washington D. C.: University of Mississippi and the Center for the Study of Southern Culture, 1982.

Lohrenz, Mary Edna, and Anita Miller. *Mississippi Homespun: Nineteenth Century Textiles and the Women Who Made Them.* Jackson, Miss.: Mississippi Department of Archives and History, 1987.

McKinney, Nancy, ed. *Traditions in Cloth: Afro-American Quilts/West African Textiles.* Los Angeles: California Afro-American Museum, 1986.

Patterns: A Celebration of Georgia's Quilting Traditions. Madison, Ga.: Madison-Morgan Cultural Center, 1990.

Ramsey, Bets, and Merikay Waldvogel. *Quilts of Tennessee: Images of Domestic Life Prior to 1930.* Nashville: Rutledge Hill Press, 1986.

Roach-Lankford, Susan, ed. *Gifts from the Hills: North Central Louisiana Folk Traditions.* Ruston, La.: Louisiana Tech University, 1984.

Robinson, Charlotte, ed. *The Artist and the Quilt.* New York: Alfred A. Knopf, 1983.

Ross, Doran H. *Fighting With Art: Appliqued Flags of the Fante Asafo.* Los Angeles: U.C.L.A. Museum of Cultural History, 1979.

Roth, Moira. *Faith Ringgold: Change: Painted Story Quilts.* New York: Bernice Steinbaum Gallery, 1987.

Seiber, Roy. *African Textiles and Decorative Arts.* New York: The Museum of Modern Art, 1973.

Southern Comfort: Quilts from the Atlanta Historical Society Collection. Atlanta: Atlanta Historical Society, 1978.

Vlach, John Michael. *The Afro-American Tradition in Decorative Arts.* Cleveland, Ohio: Cleveland Museum of Art, 1978.

Wadsworth, Anna, ed. *Missing Pieces: Georgia Folk Art, 1770-1976*. Atlanta: Georgia Council for the Arts, 1976.

Wahlman, Maude S., and Ellen King Torrey. *Ten Afro-American Quilters*. University, Miss.: The Center for the Study of Southern Culture, 1983.

Waldvogel, Merikay. *Soft Covers for Hard Times*. Nashville: Rutledge Hill Press, 1990.

Women of Courage: An Exhibition of Photographs by Judith Sedwick, Based On the Black Women Oral History Project. Boston, Mass.: Schlesinger Library, Radcliffe College, 1984.

Woods, Marianne. *Stitches in Time: A Legacy of Ozark Quilts*. Rogers, Arkansas: Rogers Historical Museum, 1986.

Unpublished Manuscripts

Chinn, Jennie A. *African-American Quilt Making Traditions: Some Assumptions Reviewed*. Kansas State Historical Society, 1991. (An essay to be published in the forthcoming June 1992 catalogue of the Kansas Quilt Project.)

Hornback, Nancy. *Faith Ringgold*. (Wichita, Kansas: Wichita State University, 1991). "An essay that focuses on the contribution made by Faith Ringgold to breaking down the hierarchical distinctions between high and low art through her quilt art." (Hornback, May 8, 1991).

The Lenders to the Exhibition

Avery Research Center for African American History & Culture, College of Charleston, Charleston, South Carolina

Cuesta Benberry, St. Louis, Missouri

Barbara Brackman, Lawrence, Kansas

Michael A. Cummings, New York, New York

Gladys East, Philadelphia, Pennsylvania

Tyrone Geter, Akron, Ohio

Carole Harris, Detroit, Michigan

Portia Robb Higgins, Louisville, Kentucky

Dorothy H. Holden, Charlottesville, Virginia

Vera Holtzman, New York, New York

Emily Hooper, Osage City, Kansas

Jean Linden, Kew Gardens, New York

Lorraine Mahan, Philadelphia, Pennsylvania

Dr. Carolyn L. Mazloomi, Cincinnati, Ohio

Richard and Suellen Meyer, Creve Coeur, Missouri

Rowland and Eleanor B. Miller, Louisville, Kentucky

Mrs. William Miller, Arrow Rock, Missouri

George and Mary Lou Harvey Mollette, Indianapolis, Indiana

Bets Ramsey, Chattanooga, Tennessee

Dorothy Nelle Sanders, Wauwatosa, Wisconsin

Smithsonian Institution, Washington, D. C.

Jim Smoote, Chicago, Illinois

Ross Trump, Medina, Ohio

George Wilbourn, Syracuse, New York

Marie Wilson, Brooklyn, New York

Robert W. Woodruff Library, Atlanta University Center, Atlanta, Georgia

Shelly Zegart, Louisville, Kentucky

Acknowledgments
The Kentucky Quilt Project, Inc.

We were helped significantly in achieving the extraordinary size and scope of this celebration by a most generous leadership gift from PHILIP MORRIS COMPANIES INC.

We are deeply grateful to the following sources of support not only for financial assistance but also for the active interest and encouragement they lent to the project:

> Mary and Barry Bingham, Sr. Fund
> Rowland and Eleanor Bingham Miller Fund
> Louisville Convention and Visitors Bureau
> Brown-Forman Corporation
> Citizens Fidelity Bank
> James Graham Brown Foundation, Inc.

Significant contributions of time, energy, and finances by Jonathan Holstein, Eleanor Miller, Dorothy West and Shelly Zegart have been crucial to the realization of this project.

From the beginning of this project Dorothy West, Business Manager, and Kathy Mitchell McGee, Project Coordinator, have been essential to every activity. Deep appreciation is also due JoAnn Gammon, Stacy Roof and Angela Messina for the constancy and strength of their commitment to this undertaking. Special thanks to David Roth, Alyssia Lazin and Theresa Mattei for their many years of association with The Kentucky Quilt Project and their significant work on this project — and to Velma Vaughan and Virginia Durkee for their invaluable assistance to Shelly Zegart and Jonathan Holstein.

Without the generous partnership of all the participating institutions, their boards of directors and staffs, this celebration would not have been possible. We want to warmly thank each institution's director for constant support of our efforts: Gail Becker, Museum of History and Science; Rita Steinberg, Kentucky Art and Craft Gallery; Peter Morrin, J. B. Speed Art Museum; and John Begley, Louisville Visual Art Association and also as representative of Zephyr Gallery.

Active community support for the project from the beginning was given by Louisville Mayor Jerry Abramson and staff, County Judge Executive David Armstrong and staff, and Eddie Webster at the Louisville Convention and Visitors Bureau. Our thanks also go to Dan Ison, Karen Brosius, Marilynn Donini and Stephanie French at Philip Morris for their confidence in the project.

Carol and Bill Butler, Elizabeth Ingber, Cathy Rasmussen, Eunice Ray, Bill Strode, Lin Willard, Jane Hopson, Rita Bodart, Tom Owen, Amy Zegart and Dorothy Alig have willingly shared their expertise.

For their generous assistance we thank W. L. Lyons Brown Foundation, Liberty National Bank, The Michael L. Cappy Foundation, Major General Dillman A. Rash, Target Stores, Fund for the Arts, Kentucky Arts Council, Polo Ralph Lauren, Mr. and Mrs. David A. Jones, Martin Weinberg, Tracy West, Jim Kurtzweil, Steve Bass, and Terri Bass.

Our special thanks to friends and colleagues in the quilt and museum worlds for their counsel and support — Cuesta Benberry, Penny McMorris, Bonnie Leman at *Quilter's Newsletter Magazine*, Meredith Schroeder at the American Quilter's Society, Sanford Smith at Sanford L. Smith & Associates, Ltd., Phyllis Tepper, Susan Flamm and Karla Friedlich at the Museum of American Folk Art, Karey Bresenhan at International Quilt Festival, Starr Kaiser, Barbara Harp and others.

No acknowledgments of support could be complete without mentioning our families, who tried to manage without us. Kenny Zegart, Rowland Miller, Cassia Holstein, Jared Holstein, Rowlie Miller, Worth Miller, Hannah Miller, Terri Zegart and Amy Zegart.

Thanks also to those whose support, because of publication deadlines, could not be included.

The Author – Acknowledgments

I wish to thank Jonathan Holstein and Shelly Zegart, whose idea it was to produce the exhibition *Always There: The African-American Presence in American Quilts*. They have given me enormous support. When Jonathan Holstein discovered the rare multi-generational African-American Perkins-Wilbourn quilt collection, my confidence in the project soared. I also want to thank Dorothy West whose superb efficiency is matched by her monumental powers of persuasion. The Kentucky Quilt Project, Inc. and the staff of the Museum of History and Science, Louisville, have been models of cooperation.

My sincere gratitude goes to Ross Trump for lending to our exhibition one of the most historically significant and extraordinary African-American quilts in America — the Keckley quilt. I do thank Doris Bowman, curator of textiles, National Museum of American History, whose loan of the Smithsonian's quilts adds a luster of historicity to the exhibition, and additionally, for her many years of personally sharing information that accelerated the progress of my study of African-American quilt history. Grateful appreciation is extended to all of the lenders of the exhibition quilts as they, too, believed in my dream of mounting a quilt exhibition that celebrated African-American quiltmakers, slave and free, young and old, male and female, urban and rural, middle-class and poor, folk artists and trained artists, southern and northern — an exhibition of inclusion, not exclusion. A special thank you to Barbara Brackman, who gave us the benefit of her quilt dating expertise to confirm, validate and otherwise put our minds at ease concerning this very important facet of producing an accurate quilt history.

The exhibition is based on many years of study and research of African-American and general quilt history. One of my earliest supporters was Dr. Julia Davis, St. Louis' foremost authority on Negro history. She made available to me her immense files, and I thank her. My life-long friend, Alma Finney and my son, George, have been ardent partisans of my work. Most of all I have been fortunate to have a large number of friends in the quilt community. It is no exaggeration to say I owe a debt of gratitude for the encouragement and information I received directly from over one hundred quilt friends, from all over the United States, Canada and England. Although I do not have space to list all of their names, I can say I am eternally grateful to them

Cuesta Benberry

The Author

Cuesta Benberry, of St. Louis, Missouri, has engaged in the study and research of quilt history for over thirty years. Since 1975, her investigations have been primarily conducted on African-American quilt history. She has written for publication numerous quilt history essays and research papers, served as a quilt research and history editor, as a consultant for quilt exhibitions and for authors, and has lectured widely in the United States and abroad. For her quilt history research, Cuesta Benberry was cited in the 17th edition of *Marquis Who's Who of American Women*, in

the 23rd edition of *Marquis Who's Who in the Midwest*, in the 11th edition of *Who's Who in the World*, and in the *Directory of African-American Folklorists*, Smithsonian Institution Office of Folklife Programs. She was elected to the Quilter's Hall of Fame in 1983. She has co-authored with Carol Crabb a book *Patchwork Pieces of Long Ago: An Anthology of Quilt Fiction*. Cuesta Benberry has a Master's degree from the University of Missouri — St. Louis.

Directors' Statement
The Kentucky Quilt Project, Inc.

The exhibition discussed in this catalogue is one of six produced by the Kentucky Quilt Project, Inc. as part of its 1991-1992 project, "Louisville Celebrates the American Quilt." The Celebration began in November, 1991, and continued through March, 1992.

The Kentucky Quilt Project was formed in 1981 to survey the state's quilts. Its original directors were Shelly Zegart, Eleanor Bingham Miller, and Eunice Sears. Katy Christopherson organized the volunteers who aided that survey. It collected data for permanent reference on more than 1,000 quilts and exhibited some of the most interesting found in *Kentucky Quilts 1800-1900*, which appeared first at the Louisville Museum of History and Science in 1983 and at 12 other museums thereafter under the auspices of the Smithsonian Institution Traveling Exhibition Service. Since 1981 groups in 48 states have undertaken quilt surveys informed by the methods and directions of The Kentucky Quilt Project. Other project activities in the 1980s included securing a Virginia Ivey quilt for Kentucky, bringing *The Artist and the Quilt* exhibition to Louisville, curating an exhibition of Kentucky quilts in Australia, and giving financial assistance to Kentucky quilt groups for special projects. It also acted as consultant for other state quilt surveys.

In 1990 the current Directors of The Kentucky Quilt Project, Shelly Zegart, Eleanor Bingham Miller and Jonathan Holstein, began to discuss an appropriate way to celebrate the 20th anniversary of the historic exhibition, *Abstract Design in American Quilts*, which opened at the Whitney Museum of American Art, New York, in 1971. The exhibition, curated by Jonathan Holstein and Gail van der Hoof, created a worldwide awareness of American quilts as designed objects. We decided a group of events which might illustrate and further the extraordinary developments in the field over the past two decades would be most beneficial. A re-creation of the Whitney exhibition was a logical starting point, as many quilt researchers and scholars, quiltmakers, collectors, and museum personnel now actively involved with quilts, never saw that original show. We planned also five other exhibitions, four conferences and additional associated events. *Abstract Design in American Quilts* at the Louisville Museum of History and Science; *A Plain Aesthetic: Lancaster Amish Quilts*, at the J. B. Speed Art Museum; *Always There: The African-American Presence in American Quilts* at the Louisville Museum of History and Science; *Quilts Now* at Zephyr Gallery; *Narrations: The Quilts of Yvonne Wells and Carolyn Mazloomi* at the Louisville Visual Art Association (Water Tower); and *Quilt Conceptions: Quilt Designs in Other Media* at the Kentucky Art and Craft Gallery.

The four conferences were designed to further quilt scholarship in specific areas. "The African-American and the American Quilt" looked at African-American quilts both in relation to the African textile tradition and as part of the mainstream of American quilt making. "Directions in Quilt Scholarship" surveyed the field past and present, discussed quilts as art historical and social objects, and looked at problems in the field. "Quilts and Collections: Public, Private and Corporate" discussed the ways quilts are seen, collected and used by individual and corporate collectors, and museums. And "Toward an International Quilt Bibliography," through the individual efforts and interactions of 15 scholars, suggested the form and directions for a potential new quilt bibliography. Other events included lectures by scholars and quilt artists, and opportunities for participants to discuss issues in the field. In addition, data and dialogues developed at the conferences will be published, and audio and visual documentation of significant events were made for permanent record.

The Directors of the Kentucky Quilt Project hope the Celebration will bring, as did *Abstract Design in American Quilts* and the Kentucky Quilt Project's survey, new perspectives and directions to quilt scholarship, understanding and appreciation.

Jonathan Holstein
Eleanor Bingham Miller
Shelly Zegart

The Directors
The Kentucky Quilt Project, Inc.

Jonathan Holstein wrote the introduction and quilt commentaries for The Kentucky Quilt Project's exhibition catalogue, *Kentucky Quilts 1800-1900* in 1983, and became a Director in 1984. His work over the past several decades, collecting, creating exhibitions, writing and lecturing, has been seminal to the current understanding and appreciation of quilts. *Abstract Design in American Quilts*, an exhibition he curated with Gail van der Hoof in 1971, showed quilts for the first time as designed objects, and is universally noted as the starting point for the contemporary interest in quilts worldwide. Many other exhibitions here and abroad drawn from their collection gave wide circulation to their vision of quilts as aesthetic objects. His writing in the field began with the catalogue of the original Whitney Museum of American Art exhibition of *Abstract Design in American Quilts*. His study of the background and design of American quilts, *The Pieced Quilt*, was published in 1973, and many articles and catalogues followed. He continues to write about quilts, and has several books underway which he hopes to finish before the next millenium.

Eleanor Bingham Miller's interest in quilts began with collecting. She was a founder of The Kentucky Quilt Project, organized in 1981 to survey her state's quilts, and has been active in all of its projects since. She is a filmmaker and a partner in Double Play Productions, New York. In Louisville, her home, she serves the community in a number of positions, including the Boards of the J. B. Speed Art Museum and the Louisville Museum of History and Science.

Shelly Zegart was a founder in 1981 of The Kentucky Quilt Project. Her initial collecting interest expanded with that state survey to a full-time professional involvement in the field. She collects, lectures, curates exhibitions, writes, advises other groups conducting state quilt surveys and sells fine quilts. Her articles have appeared in *The Quilt Digest*, *Antique Review* and other places. She has curated many exhibitions here and abroad (including an exhibition of Kentucky quilts in Australia), and lectures on all aspects of quilt history and aesthetics.